Arizona Bucket List Guide 2025

Explore the Grand Canyon State Like Never Before

DISCLAIMER

This travel guide is provided for informational purposes only. The information contained herein is believed to be accurate and reliable as of the publication date, but may be subject to change. We are not making any warranty, express or implied, with respect to the content of this guide.

Users of this guide are responsible for verifying information independently and consulting appropriate authorities and resources prior to travel. We are not liable for any loss or damage caused by the reliance on information contained in this guide.

Information regarding travel advisories, visas, health, safety, and other important considerations can change rapidly. Users are advised to check for the most up-to-date information from official government and travel industry sources before embarking on any trip.

Travel inherently involves risk, and users are responsible for making their own informed decisions and accepting any associated risks.

TABLE OF CONTENT

Chapter 1: Introduction to Arizona

1.1 Why Visit Arizona in 2025

Arizona is one of the most exciting and diverse states in the U.S., offering something for everyone. From breathtaking natural landscapes to rich cultural experiences, it's a destination that blends adventure, history, and relaxation. Whether you're planning your first trip or returning to explore more, 2025 is the perfect year to visit the Grand Canyon State.

A Land of Endless Beauty

Arizona is home to some of the most iconic sights in the world, including the Grand Canyon, one of the Seven Natural Wonders. But there's so much more. Picture yourself standing in Sedona's vibrant red rock formations, watching the sunset turn the cliffs into a fiery spectacle. Or imagine the towering saguaro cacti of the Sonoran Desert, a symbol of the American Southwest. The diversity of Arizona's landscapes—mountains, deserts, forests, and rivers—makes it a paradise for nature lovers and photographers alike.

A Perfect Blend of Adventure and Relaxation

Adventure seekers will find plenty to do here. You can hike challenging trails in the Superstition Mountains, raft the Colorado River, or explore hidden slot canyons. For those looking to relax, Arizona offers luxury spas, golf courses, and scenic drives that let you soak in the beauty without breaking a sweat.

2025 is particularly special as the state continues to invest in preserving its natural wonders and enhancing visitor experiences. New hiking trails, improved park facilities, and eco-friendly travel options are making Arizona more accessible and enjoyable than ever.

Rich Culture and History

Arizona's cultural heritage is just as impressive as its natural beauty. It's a place where Native American traditions meet Old West history. In 2025, you can explore the Navajo Nation, visit ancient cliff dwellings, or step back in time in Tombstone, the town famous for its Wild West shootouts.

The arts and music scene is thriving, with festivals celebrating everything from Native American crafts to contemporary art. Don't miss the opportunity to experience local traditions, like tribal dances or rodeos, which give you a deeper connection to the land and its people.

Year-Round Destination

Arizona is a destination for all seasons. In the winter, head to Flagstaff for skiing and cozy mountain lodges. Spring brings wildflowers to life in the desert, while summer is perfect for escaping to higher elevations like the White Mountains. Fall, with its cooler temperatures and vibrant foliage, is ideal for exploring Arizona's scenic routes and national parks.

No matter when you visit, Arizona's sunny weather and clear skies make it easy to enjoy outdoor activities and stunning stargazing opportunities.

Exciting Events in 2025

2025 is packed with events and festivals that showcase Arizona's unique culture. The Tucson Gem and Mineral Show, one of the largest in the world, attracts collectors and enthusiasts from everywhere. The Scottsdale Arabian Horse Show is a must-see for animal lovers. And the vibrant Native American festivals happening across the state give you a rare chance to experience authentic traditions and storytelling.

Accessible and Welcoming

Arizona prides itself on being a welcoming destination. It's easy to reach with major airports in Phoenix and Tucson, and the state's infrastructure makes traveling between its cities and natural wonders a breeze. Whether you're visiting as a solo traveler, a family, or a group of friends, Arizona offers options for every type of trip.

Why 2025 is the Perfect Year

Visiting Arizona in 2025 means enjoying the best of the past and the future. The state is celebrating milestones in preserving its parks and cultural landmarks. Eco-friendly travel initiatives are encouraging responsible tourism, making it easier for visitors to leave a positive impact.

So, why visit Arizona in 2025? Because it's a state that inspires awe, welcomes curiosity, and offers endless opportunities to create unforgettable memories. Get ready to explore a land where natural beauty, adventure, and culture come together in perfect harmony.

1.2 Overview of the Grand Canyon State

Arizona, famously known as the Grand Canyon State, is a land of contrasts and diversity. With its iconic desert landscapes, towering mountains, and rich cultural heritage, Arizona captures the essence of the American Southwest. Here's a closer look at what makes this state so remarkable.

Geography: A Landscape of Wonders

Arizona spans nearly 114,000 square miles, making it the sixth-largest state in the U.S. Its geography is as varied as it is stunning. To the north, the Colorado Plateau dominates with dramatic cliffs, canyons, and mesas, including the world-renowned Grand Canyon. Central Arizona is home to Sedona's red rock formations and lush forests, while the south features sprawling deserts dotted with saguaro cacti.

This diversity means Arizona has it all: arid deserts, snow-capped peaks, sparkling lakes, and dense pine forests. Whether you're a hiker, photographer, or casual traveler, the natural beauty here will leave you breathless.

History: A Rich and Layered Past

Arizona's history is deeply rooted in Native American cultures, with 22 federally recognized tribes calling the state home. Ancient ruins like Montezuma Castle and the cliff dwellings at Walnut Canyon showcase the ingenuity of early inhabitants.

In the 19th century, Arizona became a hub for Old West legends, with towns like Tombstone and Prescott preserving this fascinating era. The state officially joined the Union as the 48th state in 1912, but its cultural and historical significance stretches back thousands of years.

Climate: A State of Contrasts

Arizona's climate varies widely depending on where you are. The southern desert areas, including Phoenix and Tucson, are known for their hot summers and mild winters. Meanwhile, northern regions like Flagstaff and the White Mountains experience snowy winters and cool summers, perfect for escaping the heat.

This range of climates means you can enjoy sunbathing in the desert, skiing in the mountains, and hiking through forests—all in one trip!

People and Culture: A Blend of Old and New

Arizona is a melting pot of cultures, blending Native American, Hispanic, and Western influences. You'll find this rich heritage in the state's festivals, food, and art. Visit local markets to see Native American jewelry and crafts, or attend a rodeo to experience the Wild West spirit.

The state's urban areas, like Phoenix and Tucson, offer modern amenities and vibrant arts scenes, while smaller towns provide a glimpse into Arizona's historic and rural charm.

Economy and Tourism: What Drives Arizona

Tourism is a major part of Arizona's economy, attracting millions of visitors each year. The Grand Canyon alone draws over 5 million people annually, but attractions like Sedona, Monument Valley, and Saguaro National Park are just as captivating.

Beyond tourism, Arizona thrives on industries like agriculture, mining, and technology. Cities like Phoenix are rapidly growing hubs for innovation, offering a mix of career opportunities and cultural experiences.

Wildlife: A Nature Lover's Paradise

Arizona is home to unique and diverse wildlife. The deserts teem with creatures like roadrunners, rattlesnakes, and coyotes, while the forests are habitats for elk, black bears, and bald eagles. Birdwatchers flock to the state for its incredible variety of species, including hummingbirds and hawks.

Don't forget about the state's flora, either. The towering saguaro cactus is an iconic symbol, and during the spring, wildflowers blanket the desert in vibrant colors.

Fun Facts About Arizona

The Grand Canyon is one of the Seven Natural Wonders of the World.

Arizona does not observe Daylight Saving Time (except for the Navajo Nation).

The state has more certified dark sky locations than any other, making it a stargazer's dream.

It's home to the world's largest solar telescope at Kitt Peak National Observatory.

Why It's Called the Grand Canyon State

The nickname "Grand Canyon State" reflects Arizona's pride in its most famous natural landmark. Spanning 277 miles long and over a mile deep, the Grand Canyon is not just a geological wonder—it's a cultural and spiritual icon, especially for the Native American tribes who have lived here for centuries.

Your Gateway to Adventure

Arizona isn't just a place—it's an experience. Whether you're drawn by its natural beauty, fascinated by its history, or excited to explore its modern cities, the Grand Canyon State offers endless opportunities for adventure, learning, and inspiration.

As we delve deeper into this guide, you'll discover how to make the most of your visit to this unforgettable destination.

1.3 How to Use This Guide

Welcome to the Arizona Travel Guide 2025—your comprehensive companion to exploring the Grand Canyon State! This guide is designed to make your trip planning as easy, enjoyable, and efficient as possible. Whether you're a first-time visitor or a seasoned traveler, you'll find everything you need to create an unforgettable Arizona adventure.

Who Is This Guide For?

This guide is for anyone planning a trip to Arizona. Whether you're traveling solo, with family, or as part of a group, you'll find tailored advice for your needs. From budget-conscious travelers to luxury seekers, this book covers a wide range of experiences to suit every preference.

How This Guide Is Organized

The guide is divided into 10 chapters, each focusing on a specific aspect of Arizona travel:

Introduction to Arizona: Learn why Arizona should be on your travel radar in 2025, with a detailed overview of its history, culture, and geography.

Getting to and Around Arizona: Discover transportation options and insider tips for navigating the state efficiently.

Best Time to Visit: Understand Arizona's seasons, weather, and special events to pick the perfect time for your trip.

Top Attractions and Destinations: Explore the must-see landmarks, cities, and natural wonders.

Outdoor Adventures and Activities: Dive into Arizona's outdoor offerings, from hiking to stargazing.

Culture, History, and Local Life: Immerse yourself in the rich cultural tapestry of Arizona.

Where to Stay: Find the best accommodations, from luxury resorts to rustic cabins.

Dining and Local Flavors: Savor Arizona's unique culinary scene and local favorites.

Travel Tips and Practical Information: Get essential advice for budgeting, safety, and packing.

FAQs and Additional Resources: Address common traveler questions and find tools to enhance your trip.

Each chapter is packed with practical advice, detailed descriptions, and insider tips to help you navigate the state like a pro.

Key Features of This Guide

Practical Information: Find details on opening hours, ticket prices, contact information, and addresses for attractions, accommodations, and restaurants.

Customizable Itineraries: Use suggested itineraries to create a schedule that fits your interests and timeframe.

Up-to-Date Details: This guide includes the latest information on events, transportation, and attractions in 2025.

Insider Tips: Learn about lesser-known gems, local customs, and pro tips for avoiding crowds.

Interactive Tools: Pair this guide with travel apps and maps for a seamless experience.

How to Plan Your Trip

Here's a step-by-step way to use this guide:

Start with Chapters 1-3: Get inspired by learning about Arizona's highlights, seasons, and transportation options.

Dive into Chapters 4-5: Choose your must-see attractions and outdoor adventures.

Decide Where to Stay (Chapter 7): Find accommodations that suit your travel style and budget.

Plan Your Dining (Chapter 8): Explore Arizona's culinary landscape and note any must-visit restaurants.

Consult Chapters 9-10: Use travel tips, FAQs, and resources to finalize your plans and prepare for a smooth trip.

Navigating This Guide

Each chapter is structured to provide you with:

Highlights: Key attractions, activities, or tips to focus on.

Practical Information: Specific details to help with logistics.

Pro Tips: Local insights and recommendations to enhance your experience.

This guide is written in simple, conversational language to ensure that anyone, from seasoned travelers to first-timers, can easily follow along and feel confident about planning their trip.

Your Journey Awaits

With this guide in hand, you're well-equipped to explore Arizona's vast landscapes, vibrant cities, and cultural treasures. Let's embark on this adventure together and make your 2025 trip to Arizona truly unforgettable!

1.4 Fun Facts About Arizona

Arizona is a state full of surprises, from its quirky facts to its rich history. Here's a collection of fun and fascinating tidbits that will make you appreciate the Grand Canyon State even more:

Geographical Wonders

Home to the Grand Canyon: The Grand Canyon, one of the Seven Natural Wonders of the World, is so massive it can fit the entire state of Rhode Island within it!

Desert Beauty: Arizona is the only state where four distinct deserts converge—the Sonoran, Mojave, Chihuahuan, and Great Basin deserts.

Meteor Crater: Near Winslow, Arizona is one of the best-preserved meteor impact sites on Earth, formed over 50,000 years ago.

Rivers in the Desert: Despite its arid reputation, Arizona is home to two major rivers, the Colorado and the Gila, providing water to millions.

History and Culture

Oldest Continuously Inhabited City: Oraibi, a Hopi village, has been inhabited since around 1100 AD, making it one of the oldest continuously occupied settlements in North America.

Native American Influence: Arizona is home to 22 federally recognized tribes, with more Native American land than any other state.

Copper State: Arizona is the leading producer of copper in the U.S., with enough copper mined annually to make 2.6 million miles of copper wire!

Tombstone's Legendary Shootout: The town of Tombstone is famous for the gunfight at the O.K. Corral, a hallmark of the Wild West era.

Unique Wildlife and Plants

Saguaro Cactus: Found only in the Sonoran Desert, this iconic cactus can grow over 40 feet tall and live up to 200 years.

Wildlife Diversity: Arizona is home to animals ranging from javelinas and Gila monsters to elk and bald eagles.

Hummingbird Haven: Arizona boasts more hummingbird species than any other state, with over 15 varieties visiting annually.

Weather and Climate

No Daylight Saving Time: Arizona (except for the Navajo Nation) does not observe Daylight Saving Time, making life here simpler for locals and travelers alike.

Sunshine Galore: Arizona averages over 300 sunny days a year, making it one of the sunniest places in the United States.

Snowy Peaks: Despite its desert reputation, Flagstaff sees an average of 100 inches of snow each year, offering great skiing opportunities.

Quirky Facts

London Bridge Relocated: The London Bridge was dismantled in the UK and rebuilt in Lake Havasu City, Arizona, in 1971.

Planetary Research Hub: The University of Arizona played a key role in developing the Mars Rover and other space missions.

Official State Neckwear: Arizona's official state neckwear is the bolo tie, a nod to its Western heritage.

Tourism and Travel

Certified Dark Skies: Arizona has more certified dark sky communities and parks than any other state, making it a stargazing paradise.

Route 66: A significant stretch of historic Route 66 runs through Arizona, offering a nostalgic journey through Americana.

Natural Hot Springs: The state has numerous natural hot springs, perfect for relaxing in a stunning setting.

Pop Culture and Trivia

Hollywood Favorite: Movies like Stagecoach and 3:10 to Yuma were filmed in Arizona's dramatic landscapes.

UFO Capital: Arizona is famous for the 1997 "Phoenix Lights" UFO sighting, one of the most talked-about unexplained phenomena in the U.S.

State Gemstone: Turquoise is Arizona's official gemstone, celebrated for its vibrant blue hues and cultural significance.

Did You Know?

Arizona was the last of the contiguous 48 states to join the Union, achieving statehood on February 14, 1912—making it a Valentine's Day state!

Prescott, Arizona, was the original territorial capital before Phoenix took over in 1889.

The state's Petrified Forest National Park features fossils dating back over 200 million years.

These fun facts are just a glimpse into Arizona's unique character. As you explore the state, you'll uncover even more reasons to marvel at this incredible destination.

Chapter 2: Getting to and Around Arizona

2.1 Transportation Options (Air, Car, Train, and Bus)

When traveling to Arizona, there are various ways to get there and explore the state. Whether you're flying in from another part of the U.S. or driving cross-country, Arizona is well-connected and easy to navigate. Below are the key transportation options to consider:

Air Travel

Arizona is served by several major airports, with Phoenix Sky Harbor International Airport (PHX) being the state's busiest and largest airport. It's conveniently located just minutes from downtown Phoenix, and it offers flights to and from destinations across the globe.

Other Major Airports in Arizona:

Tucson International Airport (TUS): Located in southern Arizona, it's the second-largest airport in the state, offering flights from major U.S. cities.
Sedona Airport (SEZ): For those visiting Sedona, the small but scenic Sedona Airport is just 5 miles from the town center and is known for its stunning views and small plane traffic.

Flagstaff Pulliam Airport (FLG): Ideal for those heading to the northern part of the state, Flagstaff's airport is a great access point for the Grand Canyon and other northern attractions.

Airlines and Fares:

Major airlines such as American Airlines, Southwest, United, and Delta provide regular services to Arizona's main airports.

Airfare prices vary greatly depending on the season and how far in advance you book. On average, round-trip domestic flights can range from $150 to $400, with international fares starting from $600 or more.

Getting to Your Destination from the Airport:

Rental Cars: Available at all major airports. Expect to pay around $40–$100 per day, depending on the car type and rental agency.

Taxis & Rideshares: Ride services like Uber and Lyft are available at all major airports and can cost anywhere from $15 to $50 depending on the distance to your destination.

Shuttle Services: Many hotels offer shuttle services, and there are also shuttle companies that service popular tourist destinations. Rates typically range from $20 to $50 per person, depending on the distance.

Car Rental

Renting a car is one of the best ways to explore Arizona, especially if you plan to visit places outside the major cities, such as national parks, rural areas, or scenic byways. The state offers a variety of landscapes and natural wonders that are best experienced with the freedom of your own vehicle.

Rental Car Companies:

Major rental agencies like Enterprise, Hertz, Budget, Avis, and Alamo are readily available at airports and local locations throughout Arizona.

Prices typically range from $25 to $50 per day for an economy car, while larger vehicles like SUVs or minivans can cost $60–$100 per day. Rental prices may fluctuate based on demand, especially during peak tourist seasons (spring and fall).

Driving Tips:

Roads and Highways: Arizona has a well-maintained network of highways and interstates, making it easy to drive around. Be mindful of the desert landscape, especially during the summer months, when heat and dry conditions can be intense.

Speed Limits: Speed limits are typically 65-75 mph on highways and 25-35 mph in cities. Pay attention to posted signs.

Desert Driving: If you're driving in rural desert areas, carry plenty of water, have a charged phone, and make sure your vehicle is in good condition. Gas stations may be far apart in some remote areas.

Train Travel

While Arizona doesn't have a comprehensive train network, Amtrak provides service to several cities in the state, offering scenic and leisurely routes.

Amtrak Routes:

The Southwest Chief: Travels from Chicago to Los Angeles, stopping in Flagstaff and Winslow. This is a popular option for travelers headed to northern Arizona, including the Grand Canyon.

The Sunset Limited: This route travels between New Orleans and Los Angeles, stopping in Tucson.

Cost and Duration:

Prices for train travel can vary based on the route and class of service, with tickets ranging from $50 to $150 or more.

Amtrak trains offer sleeper cars, dining options, and ample space to relax, but travel times can be longer than flying or driving.

Station Locations:

Flagstaff Amtrak Station (FLG): Serving the northern part of the state.

Tucson Amtrak Station (TUS): Located in southern Arizona, ideal for accessing the southern regions of the state.

Bus Travel

Bus services are an affordable way to travel around Arizona, especially for budget-conscious visitors. Several companies provide interstate and regional bus routes, including Greyhound and FlixBus.

Greyhound:

Routes: Connects major Arizona cities, including Phoenix, Tucson, and Flagstaff, to other U.S. cities.

Price: Bus tickets can be very affordable, starting from as low as $10 to $50, depending on the route and how early you book.

Travel Time: Bus travel can be slower compared to other transportation methods, with journeys taking several hours for long distances.

Stations: Bus stations are located in downtown areas and are often close to other forms of public transport, such as light rail or city buses.

FlixBus:

A newer, budget-friendly option that connects Phoenix with cities like Tucson and Flagstaff. It offers comfortable buses, free Wi-Fi, and affordable ticket prices.

Tickets: Start as low as $5 for shorter routes, with longer routes typically costing around $20–$40.

Public Transport Within Cities

Once you're in Arizona's cities, there are various public transportation options to help you get around.

Phoenix: The Valley Metro operates buses, light rail, and commuter rail throughout the Phoenix metro area. The light rail connects downtown Phoenix with Tempe and Mesa.

Fares: Bus fare is $2 for a 2-hour pass, and light rail tickets are $2 for a single ride.

Passes: Day passes are available for $4, and monthly passes cost around $64.

Tucson: The Sun Tran bus system serves Tucson and is the best way to navigate the city.

Fares: Single ride fare is $1.75, and a 1-day pass costs $4.

Conclusion

With a variety of transportation options available, you can easily access Arizona's major cities, attractions, and hidden gems. Whether you prefer the flexibility of renting a car, the convenience of flying, or the slower pace of train or bus travel, Arizona offers diverse ways to get around. Plan ahead, choose the best option for your trip, and enjoy your Arizona adventure!

2.2 Driving Tips and Scenic Routes

Arizona's diverse landscapes—from desert expanses to towering mountain peaks—make it a dream destination for road trips. The state offers some of the most beautiful scenic drives in the U.S., but driving through Arizona's terrain can also present unique challenges. Here's everything you need to know to make your road trip smooth and enjoyable.

Driving Tips for Arizona

Before hitting the open road in Arizona, there are a few important driving tips to keep in mind:

1. Prepare for the Weather

Summer Heat: Arizona is known for its scorching summers, especially in cities like Phoenix and Tucson. Temperatures can easily reach over 100°F (38°C) during the day.

Tip: Always keep a bottle of water in your car and make sure your vehicle's air conditioning is working properly. If you're driving in remote areas, carry extra water in case of emergencies.

Desert Terrain: The vast desert landscapes can be deceptive, and the roads may stretch for miles without any signs of civilization.

Tip: Make sure your vehicle is in good condition, with a full gas tank, and that you have a charged phone in case you need assistance.

Winter Roads: If you're traveling to northern Arizona during the winter, be prepared for snow and icy conditions, especially in places like Flagstaff and the Grand Canyon.

Tip: Check road conditions before traveling, and consider renting a vehicle with snow tires if you'll be in mountainous areas during winter months.

2. Speed Limits

Arizona's highways and interstates have speed limits that are typically higher than those in many other states. However, always keep an eye out for posted speed limit signs, as they can vary based on location and road conditions.

Speed Limits:

Interstate highways: 65-75 mph

City streets: 25-35 mph

Rural roads: 55 mph, though it can be lower in certain areas

3. Watch for Wildlife

Arizona is home to a variety of wildlife, from desert animals like coyotes and javelinas to larger creatures like elk and deer in the northern and mountainous areas.

Tip: Always be on the lookout for wildlife, especially when driving at night. Deer and elk are most active during dawn and dusk.

4. Rest Stops and Gas Stations

In more remote parts of Arizona, gas stations and rest stops can be spaced out by long distances. Make sure to fill up when you have the chance, particularly if you're traveling along routes like I-40 or US-93.

Tip: Plan your gas stops and take breaks at rest areas to avoid driving too long without refueling. Always have a physical map on hand, just in case cell service drops.

Scenic Routes to Explore in Arizona

Arizona is famous for its scenic byways that allow visitors to take in the stunning natural beauty of the state. Here are some of the most spectacular drives:

1. The Grand Canyon's Desert View Drive

One of the most iconic drives in the state, Desert View Drive takes you along the South Rim of the Grand Canyon. The route stretches for 25 miles (40 km) from Grand Canyon Village to Desert View Watchtower.

What to Expect: Expect breathtaking views of the Grand Canyon's vastness, with several scenic overlooks along the way, including the popular Grandview Point.
Highlights: Desert View Watchtower, panoramic canyon views, and the Colorado River in the distance.

When to Go: Best during the spring or fall, when temperatures are cooler and the crowds are smaller.

2. Route 66 (Historic Arizona Route)

The historic Route 66 runs across Arizona and offers a nostalgic journey through desert landscapes, small towns, and quirky roadside attractions. The route stretches from the New Mexico border to the California border, passing through cities like Flagstaff, Winslow, and Seligman.

What to Expect: You'll drive through colorful desert towns, stop at retro diners, and see fascinating landmarks like the Meteor Crater and the Wigwam Motel.

Highlights: Historic Route 66 landmarks, Petrified Forest National Park, and the famous "Standin' on the Corner" in Winslow, Arizona.

3. The Scenic Drive on State Route 89A (Sedona to Flagstaff)

This route takes you from the red rock town of Sedona to the cool pines of Flagstaff, passing through Oak Creek Canyon. It's one of the most picturesque drives in Arizona.

What to Expect: Stunning views of red rock formations, switchback roads, and towering trees as you climb toward the higher elevations of Flagstaff.

Highlights: Oak Creek Canyon, scenic overlooks, and opportunities to stop for short hikes.

When to Go: This route is spectacular year-round, but especially in the fall when the changing leaves provide a burst of color against the red rocks.

4. The Kitt Peak Scenic Drive

Located south of Tucson, this route takes you to Kitt Peak National Observatory, one of the world's largest astronomical observatories. The road to Kitt Peak offers panoramic views of the surrounding desert and mountains.

What to Expect: A winding, 12-mile road leading up to the observatory, offering stunning vistas of the Sonoran Desert.

Highlights: The observatory itself, which houses the world's largest collection of optical telescopes. You can also take a guided tour of the observatory.

When to Go: Sunrise or sunset, when the views are especially dramatic.

5. The Apache Trail (State Route 88)

This is a historic and rugged drive that takes you through the Superstition Mountains to the historic mining town of Globe. The Apache Trail winds through desert terrain, providing access to some of Arizona's most scenic lakes and canyons.

What to Expect: A narrow, winding road with steep grades and sharp curves, which requires cautious driving. Be prepared for breathtaking desert views and the opportunity to stop at Goldfield Ghost Town and Canyon Lake.

Highlights: Lost Dutchman State Park, Superstition Mountains, Goldfield Ghost Town, and Canyon Lake.

When to Go: Ideal during spring or fall when the temperatures are milder.

6. The Coronado Trail Scenic Byway (US 191)

Located in southeastern Arizona, this route is perfect for those looking for an adventurous drive with some of the most beautiful views in the state. The route takes you from the Arizona-Mexico border up to the White Mountains.

What to Expect: You'll travel through the rugged and mountainous terrain of the Apache-Sitgreaves National Forest, offering amazing opportunities for wildlife watching and photography.

Highlights: The unique mix of desert and mountainous landscapes, plus the chance to visit the historic Coronado National Memorial.

When to Go: Best in late spring or early fall for comfortable temperatures and clear skies.

Conclusion

Driving in Arizona is more than just a way to get from one place to another—it's an adventure in itself. From scenic desert highways to winding mountain roads, Arizona offers unforgettable drives for every type of traveler. Whether you're looking to explore national parks, experience local culture, or simply enjoy the open road, Arizona's highways are ready to take you on an incredible journey. Make sure to plan your route, keep an eye on the weather, and enjoy the stunning landscapes along the way!

2.3 Local Public Transport

While Arizona is best known for its vast landscapes and scenic drives, public transportation can be a convenient and affordable way to explore some areas, particularly in larger cities like Phoenix, Tucson, and Flagstaff. Whether you're hopping on a bus, taking the light rail, or exploring a more local transportation option, here's what you need to know about getting around via public transport in Arizona.

1. Buses in Arizona

Arizona's public bus systems are well-established, especially in urban areas. Buses are typically affordable and a great option if you're staying in or near the main cities. Here's a look at what each major city offers:

Phoenix

Valley Metro operates the bus system in Phoenix, serving both the city and surrounding areas. With routes covering the entire metro area, Valley Metro buses are a popular and budget-friendly option.

Fares: A one-way fare costs around $2.00, with discounts for seniors, students, and those with disabilities. You can also purchase a day pass for $4.00 or a monthly pass for $64.00.

Where to Go: Popular routes take you through downtown Phoenix, to the Phoenix Sky Harbor Airport, to major attractions like the Desert Botanical Garden and Heard Museum, and to areas like Tempe and Scottsdale.

Tucson

Sun Tran operates Tucson's bus system, providing reliable service throughout the city and surrounding neighborhoods.

Fares: A one-way fare is typically around $1.75. A day pass costs about $3.00, and monthly passes are available for $48.00.

Where to Go: Sun Tran buses reach key locations such as the University of Arizona, the Tucson International Airport, downtown Tucson, and shopping centers like Park Place Mall.

Flagstaff

Mountain Line serves Flagstaff, offering bus services throughout the city and into nearby areas.

Fares: One-way fare costs about $1.50, with discounts available for seniors and students. There are also day passes and multi-ride options.

Where to Go: The bus system can take you to Northern Arizona University, the Flagstaff Mall, and around downtown Flagstaff. During the winter season, Mountain Line provides routes to Arizona Snowbowl, a popular ski resort.

2. Light Rail

In addition to buses, light rail is an efficient and convenient way to get around, especially in Phoenix. The Valley Metro Light Rail connects Phoenix with neighboring Tempe and Mesa, making it a great option for travelers heading to cultural destinations, sporting events, and local attractions.

Phoenix Light Rail:

Fares: A one-way fare costs $2.00, with a day pass available for $4.00. Monthly passes are also available for regular commuters.

What to Expect: The light rail operates along a 26-mile stretch, with stops at major locations like the Heard Museum, Chase Field, Phoenix Convention Center, and Arizona State University in Tempe. It's a great way to avoid traffic and quickly travel to popular spots without worrying about parking.

3. Ride-Sharing and Taxis

In addition to traditional public transportation, ride-sharing services like Uber and Lyft are widely available in Arizona, particularly in urban areas like Phoenix and Tucson. These options can be convenient if you're traveling shorter distances or need a more direct route to a specific location.

Ride-sharing: Both Uber and Lyft operate in many cities in Arizona. Rates will vary depending on distance, traffic, and demand, but they typically charge around $1-$2 per mile plus a base fare.

Taxis: While ride-sharing is often more convenient, taxis are also available. Rates typically start at $2.00 and increase with distance, along with any additional charges like waiting time.

4. Bicycles and Pedestrian Accessibility

For those looking for a more eco-friendly way to explore cities, Arizona offers several bike-sharing programs and pedestrian-friendly pathways, especially in cities like Phoenix and Tucson.

Bike Rentals:

Grid Bikes in Phoenix and Tucson Bike Share offer easy access to bikes for short trips around the city. These bike-share programs allow you to rent bikes by the hour or day.

Fares: Bike rental costs typically range from $1.00 for 30 minutes to $8.00 for a full day of rental.

Pedestrian Walkways:

Arizona cities, especially Phoenix and Tucson, have made efforts to improve walkability, with dedicated pedestrian pathways in key areas. The best pedestrian-friendly zones are in the downtown areas, university districts, and near major attractions.

5. Limited Public Transport in Rural Areas

While public transportation options in Arizona's larger cities are extensive, rural areas of the state may have limited service. In more remote locations, such as small towns and rural areas in the north and east of the state, you may find few or no public transport options available.

Tip: If you're heading into rural areas or national parks, renting a car is the best option for flexibility and convenience. For those staying in small towns, it's advisable to plan your travel around local services, as public transport may be infrequent.

Conclusion

Whether you're relying on buses, light rail, or taxis, Arizona's public transportation systems provide an affordable and convenient way to explore its major cities. For those looking to travel beyond the urban areas, however, renting a car or using a ride-sharing service is likely your best bet. Make sure to plan your routes ahead of time, especially if you're exploring outside of major cities, as public transport options may be more limited in rural areas.

2.4 Navigating Rural and Urban Areas

Arizona offers a unique blend of urban landscapes and vast rural expanses, each with its own set of challenges and advantages when it comes to navigating. Whether you're exploring the bustling city streets or venturing into the serene deserts and mountains of the state's rural areas, it's important to understand the best ways to get around each environment. Here's what you need to know about navigating both rural and urban Arizona.

Urban Areas: Navigating the Cities

Arizona's major cities, such as Phoenix, Tucson, Mesa, and Scottsdale, are well-developed with ample transportation options. These cities are known for their spread-out layouts and traffic congestion, especially during rush hours. Here are some tips for navigating urban areas efficiently:

1. Traffic and Parking

Rush Hour: In cities like Phoenix, rush hour (7:00 AM - 9:00 AM and 4:00 PM - 6:00 PM) can lead to heavy traffic, especially on main roads like Interstate 10 and Loop 101. Be prepared for delays, and consider avoiding peak times if possible.

The Apache Trail: For a more rugged experience, head along the Apache Trail, a 40-mile route through the Superstition Mountains. While it's a bit off the beaten path, it's worth it for its scenic beauty and historical significance.

The Scenic Byways: Arizona boasts several scenic byways that offer incredible views, such as the Red Rock Scenic Byway (near Sedona) and the Coronado Trail in southeastern Arizona. These routes will take you past some of the most picturesque scenery in the state.

5. Navigating Arizona's Parks and Natural Wonders

Many of Arizona's most popular natural attractions, like the Grand Canyon, Petrified Forest, and Saguaro National Park, are located in remote areas. To make the most of your visit:

Maps and Signage: Most of Arizona's parks are well-marked with signs, and you'll find plenty of maps at park entrances. However, if you plan to hike or explore off the beaten path, it's a good idea to download trail maps or take a printed version with you.

Tourist Information Centers: Many parks and visitor centers offer free maps and guidance on the best routes. Stop by to get the most up-to-date information on conditions, road closures, and recommended routes.

Conclusion

Navigating both rural and urban Arizona requires some planning, but it's an adventure worth undertaking. While major cities offer a wealth of public transportation options, Arizona's expansive rural areas demand a bit more effort, particularly in terms of driving and preparation. Whether you're exploring the state's urban centers or venturing into the vast desert and mountains, make sure to plan ahead, check road conditions, and stay safe on your journey.

2.5 Accessibility Options for Travelers

Arizona is a destination that caters to a wide range of travelers, including those with mobility challenges or other accessibility needs. Whether you're visiting its vibrant cities, stunning national parks, or remote rural areas, the state offers various options to ensure that everyone can enjoy its natural beauty and attractions comfortably and safely.

1. Accessible Transportation

Public Transit

Phoenix: The Valley Metro light rail system and buses are equipped with ramps and other accessibility features for passengers with mobility impairments. The light rail stations and buses have been designed to be wheelchair-friendly, and the trains feature space for wheelchairs and mobility devices.

Tucson: The Sun Tran bus system also provides accessible buses with ramps and designated spaces for wheelchairs and strollers. Many bus stops have paved surfaces for easy access, and there are digital displays to help with navigation for people with visual impairments.

For both cities, services can be tracked via apps, so you can plan your trips easily while on the move. Some areas also offer paratransit services for those who cannot use regular public transportation.

Taxis and Ride-sharing

In Arizona, ride-sharing services like Uber and Lyft are available in major cities, and some vehicles can be requested with wheelchair access. It's essential to use the app to check for accessible vehicle options in your area. There are also local taxi services in larger cities like Phoenix and Tucson with accessible cabs for passengers with mobility needs.

Car Rentals

Many rental agencies in Arizona offer vehicles equipped with hand controls or other modifications for drivers with disabilities. Major car rental companies such as Enterprise, Hertz, and Avis provide accessible options, but it's recommended to book in advance and confirm the availability of these vehicles before your trip.

2. Accessible Hotels and Lodging

Many hotels, resorts, and inns across Arizona offer rooms designed for travelers with accessibility needs. Features in accessible rooms typically include:

Wide Doorways and Hallways: These are designed to accommodate wheelchairs or walkers.

Roll-in Showers: Many hotels provide bathrooms with roll-in showers and grab bars.

Accessible Amenities: Some hotels offer things like accessible parking spaces, elevators, and ramps for easy access to entrances and other amenities. For example, in larger cities like Phoenix, many upscale hotels offer specialized rooms for mobility-impaired guests.

Popular hotels with accessible options include:

The Arizona Biltmore, Phoenix: A luxury resort with accessible rooms, ramps, and elevators.

The Westin La Paloma Resort & Spa, Tucson: Offering accessible rooms and facilities including a pool lift.

Red Feather Lodge, Grand Canyon: Located near the Grand Canyon, this lodge has accessible rooms and parking.

It's important to contact the hotel directly when booking to confirm specific accessibility features to meet your needs.

3. Accessible Attractions and Parks

Arizona's national parks and outdoor attractions are becoming more inclusive, offering improved accessibility for all visitors, including those with mobility issues.

Grand Canyon National Park

South Rim: The South Rim of the Grand Canyon has made great strides in making the park accessible. Most of the key viewpoints and facilities along the Rim Trail are wheelchair accessible, and the Hermit Road shuttle service offers accessible buses with space for wheelchairs.

Grand Canyon Railway: For those who wish to visit the Grand Canyon via train, the Grand Canyon Railway provides accessible cars and services, including wheelchair lifts at the station.

Saguaro National Park

The park offers paved trails like the Desert Ecology Trail, which is wheelchair accessible. The visitor centers at both the Rincon Mountain District and the Tucson Mountain District also have wheelchair accessibility, including ramps and restrooms.

Sedona

Many of Sedona's hiking trails have been improved to accommodate wheelchairs, including the Bell Rock Pathway and Red Rock Scenic Byway. Sedona also offers accessible services for those with hearing or visual impairments, such as guided tours with sign language interpreters by request.

Lake Havasu State Park

The park offers accessible trails for wheelchairs and mobility devices, such as the Lakeview Trail, and accessible picnic areas and restrooms throughout the park. The London Bridge in Lake Havasu City also has accessible paths leading to and around it.

4. Accessible Outdoor Activities

Arizona is known for its outdoor activities, and there are plenty of ways to experience the state's natural wonders regardless of physical ability.

Hiking and Nature Walks

Many parks and trails in Arizona are now accessible for those in wheelchairs or with limited mobility. The Sonoran Desert has trails that offer easy-to-navigate paths, and many are wheelchair-friendly, such as the Desert Ecology Trail at Saguaro National Park. Additionally, some organizations offer adaptive hiking tours using all-terrain wheelchairs.

Adaptive Sports

Arizona is home to several organizations offering adaptive sports for individuals with disabilities, including skiing, rock climbing, and more. Arizona Disabled Sports in the Phoenix area offers programs for those with physical or developmental disabilities, from water skiing on Lake Pleasant to snowboarding at Snowbowl.

Fishing and Boating

For those who love the water, many Arizona lakes, including Lake Powell, Lake Havasu, and Lyman Lake, offer accessible docks, fishing piers, and boat rentals with adaptive equipment. If you want to try kayaking or canoeing, some outfitters provide adaptive kayaks, which allow individuals with physical disabilities to enjoy the water in a safe and comfortable way.

5. Accessible Services for Visitors with Disabilities

Several services are available for visitors to Arizona with disabilities:

Arizona Department of Transportation (ADOT): ADOT offers resources and guidance for disabled travelers, including information about accessible rest areas and services across the state. You can also find information about parking permits and how to apply for a disabled parking placard if you plan to rent or drive your own vehicle.

Visitor Centers: Many of Arizona's visitor centers provide services to travelers with disabilities, including accessible restrooms, ramps, and helpful staff who can provide detailed information about accessible routes and activities. Be sure to ask at any center you visit if you need assistance.

Conclusion

Whether you're visiting Arizona's iconic natural landscapes, experiencing its rich cultural history, or exploring its urban centers, there are many accessible options for travelers with mobility challenges. Arizona is a destination that strives to ensure every visitor can enjoy its beauty and adventure. Be sure to plan ahead, use the available resources, and make use of the accessible amenities so you can make the most of your trip to the Grand Canyon State.

Chapter 3: Best Time to Visit

3.1 Seasonal Highlights (Spring, Summer, Fall, Winter)

Arizona offers something unique in every season, making it a great destination year-round. The diverse landscape, from the deserts to the mountains, provides different experiences depending on the time of year you visit. Here's a breakdown of what to expect in each season to help you plan the perfect Arizona adventure.

Spring (March to May)
Why Visit in Spring: Spring is one of the most popular times to visit Arizona. The weather is mild, with daytime temperatures ranging from the 60s to 80s (°F), making it perfect for outdoor activities. This is also the time when the desert comes alive with wildflowers, creating colorful vistas, especially in areas like Saguaro National Park and the Sonoran Desert.

Highlights:
Wildflower Blooms: Arizona's desert landscapes transform in spring with vibrant wildflowers. The Cactus Flower Festival in Phoenix and wildflower trails in Catalina State Park offer fantastic photo opportunities.

Hiking and Outdoor Activities: This is the perfect time for hiking and exploring Arizona's many parks, including the Grand Canyon, Sedona, and Mount Lemmon. The weather is comfortable for outdoor adventures without the extreme heat that comes in summer.

Events and Festivals: Arizona hosts various festivals in spring, such as the Arizona Renaissance Festival and Tucson Folk Festival. These events provide a great chance to enjoy local food, music, and culture.
What to Pack:
Light layers for daytime warmth and a jacket for cooler evenings.
Comfortable shoes for outdoor activities like hiking.
Sunscreen and sunglasses, as the sun can be strong even in spring.
Summer (June to August)

Why Visit in Summer: Arizona summers can be scorching hot, especially in the desert regions, where temperatures often exceed 100°F (38°C). However, the high elevations, such as the Grand Canyon, Flagstaff, and Sedona, offer cooler temperatures and are great escapes from the desert heat. Additionally, summer is a perfect time for those interested in water activities at lakes and rivers.

Highlights:
Cooler Mountain Regions: If you prefer escaping the heat, head to Arizona's higher elevations like Flagstaff, Prescott, or Payson for temperatures that remain comfortable in the 70s and 80s (°F).

Water Activities: Arizona is home to several stunning lakes, such as Lake Powell, Lake Havasu, and Lake Pleasant, where you can enjoy boating, kayaking, fishing, and swimming.

Monsoon Season: Late summer brings the monsoon rains, which are often dramatic but brief. These rains provide a refreshing change to the dry desert landscape and are a unique experience for visitors, though they can cause temporary disruptions to outdoor plans.

Summer Festivals: Arizona hosts various summer festivals like the Tucson Gem and Mineral Show and Arizona Diamondbacks baseball games. These are fun ways to engage with the local culture and traditions.

What to Pack:
Light, breathable clothing to stay cool in the heat.
Hat and sunscreen to protect from the intense sun.
Water bottle to stay hydrated while exploring.
A light jacket if you plan to visit higher elevations or early mornings when temperatures drop.

Fall (September to November)
Why Visit in Fall: Fall is one of the best times to visit Arizona, as the weather is mild, and the crowds from summer begin to thin out. The daytime temperatures are generally in the 70s and 80s (°F), making it ideal for hiking, sightseeing, and

enjoying the outdoors. Fall also offers stunning fall foliage, especially in northern Arizona's forests.

Highlights:

Fall Foliage: Northern Arizona, particularly the Aspen forests of Flagstaff and Sedona, sees vibrant fall colors in October and November. The changing leaves provide a scenic backdrop for hiking and photography.

Hiking and Exploring: With the cooler temperatures and fewer crowds, fall is a fantastic time to explore the hiking trails of Grand Canyon National Park, Sedona, and Saguaro National Park. The weather is perfect for outdoor exploration.

What to Pack:

Light layers for daytime, with a jacket or sweater for cooler evenings.

Hiking boots or shoes for outdoor exploration.

A camera to capture the breathtaking fall colors.

Winter (December to February)

Why Visit in Winter: Arizona winters are generally mild, especially compared to many parts of the U.S. The desert areas remain cool, with temperatures ranging from the 50s to 60s (°F) during the day, while the higher elevations experience snow and winter sports activities. This makes winter a great time for both outdoor adventure and relaxation.

Highlights:

Skiing and Snowboarding: Arizona offers skiing at the Arizona Snowbowl near Flagstaff and Sunrise Park Resort in the White Mountains. These resorts offer a variety of slopes for all skill levels.

Winter Hiking and Scenic Drives: Winter is also a fantastic time for hiking in Arizona's desert parks, where temperatures are cooler, and the crowds are minimal. You can also enjoy scenic drives like the Route 66 or Red Rock Scenic Byway in Sedona, where the crisp air makes for a refreshing experience.

Holiday Events: Arizona celebrates the holiday season with festive events like the Glendale Glitters holiday lights display and the Tucson Parade of Lights. It's a great time to enjoy the local holiday traditions and decorations.

What to Pack:

Warm clothing, especially if you plan to visit the mountains for skiing or other winter activities.

A jacket, hat, and gloves for the cooler temperatures, especially in higher elevations. Sunscreen, as the sun can still be strong, even in winter.

Conclusion

Each season in Arizona brings its own special charm, offering different experiences depending on your interests and preferences. Whether you're visiting to hike the Grand Canyon, enjoy the cooler mountain temperatures, take part in a festival, or relax by a lake, Arizona is a year-round destination. Consider the weather, activities, and events available during your preferred time to visit, and you'll have an unforgettable trip to the Grand Canyon State.

3.2 Weather Considerations

Arizona is known for its diverse climate, ranging from desert heat to snow-capped mountains. Understanding the weather before your visit is crucial to making the most of your trip, as it can vary significantly depending on the region and time of year.

Desert Regions (Phoenix, Tucson, Yuma)

The desert regions of Arizona experience hot summers and mild winters. Daytime temperatures during summer months (June to August) often soar above 100°F (38°C), and sometimes reach up to 115°F (46°C), especially in areas like Phoenix and Yuma. However, the evenings can be cooler and more comfortable. Winter temperatures are typically mild, ranging from the mid-50s to mid-60s (°F) during the day, with nights being cooler.

Tips for Visiting:

Summer: Be prepared for the intense heat during summer. Wear lightweight, breathable clothing, carry plenty of water, and avoid outdoor activities during the hottest part of the day (usually between 10 a.m. and 4 p.m.).

Winter: The mild winter weather makes this a great time to explore the desert and engage in outdoor activities, such as hiking or cycling.

Mountain Regions (Flagstaff, Sedona, Prescott)

Arizona's higher elevations, like Flagstaff and Sedona, experience more temperate climates. Summer in these areas is much cooler compared to the desert, with daytime temperatures ranging from the 70s to 80s (°F). Winter, however, can bring cold temperatures and even snow, especially in Flagstaff, which is known for being the state's snowiest city. The average winter temperature is between 30°F to 50°F (0°C to 10°C), but snowstorms are common, making this a perfect winter wonderland for snow sports enthusiasts.

Tips for Visiting:
Summer: Temperatures in mountain areas are pleasant and ideal for hiking, camping, and outdoor exploration. Be sure to bring layers, as temperatures can change rapidly.
Winter: If you're planning to ski or snowboard, pack warm layers, waterproof clothing, and snow gear. Be prepared for snowy roads and check the weather before heading out.

Northern and High Elevation Regions (Grand Canyon, White Mountains)
Northern Arizona, home to the Grand Canyon and the White Mountains, experiences cooler weather year-round. Summer temperatures in these areas range from the 70s to 80s (°F) during the day, with cooler nights. Winter can be quite cold, especially at the Grand Canyon, where temperatures regularly fall below freezing. The Grand Canyon can receive heavy snow, which can make it a winter wonderland. The White Mountains and Arizona Snowbowl are also popular destinations for snow sports.

Tips for Visiting:
Summer: Summer is a fantastic time to explore the Grand Canyon and its trails, as temperatures are mild compared to the desert. However, don't forget to pack a hat, sunscreen, and enough water.

Winter: If visiting during winter, prepare for cold and potentially snowy conditions. Make sure to dress warmly and check weather forecasts for any road closures or storm warnings.

Rain and Monsoon Seasons

Arizona's monsoon season, which occurs from June to September, brings heavy rainfall and thunderstorms, especially in the southern and central regions. Although it only lasts for a short period, the monsoon rains can dramatically change the landscape, offering cooler temperatures and dramatic skies. While this season isn't ideal for outdoor hiking or camping, it is a fascinating time to witness the desert come alive with lush vegetation and temporary waterfalls.

Tips for Visiting During Monsoon Season:

Be prepared for sudden rain showers and flash flooding, especially in desert areas and canyon regions. If hiking, make sure to stay on marked trails, and check the weather forecast for storms.

Pack an umbrella or rain jacket to stay dry if you're exploring the cities or towns during these months.

3.3 Events and Festivals

Arizona is a state that loves to celebrate its culture, history, and natural beauty. The state hosts a wide variety of events and festivals throughout the year, each offering a unique way to experience Arizona's charm.

Spring Events
Tucson Festival of Books (March)
 This beloved festival attracts book lovers from across the country. It features hundreds of authors, panel discussions, and book signings, as well as educational programs for families. The event takes place on the beautiful campus of the University of Arizona.

Arizona Renaissance Festival (February to April)
 Step back in time at this medieval festival, complete with jousting tournaments, theatrical performances, artisan vendors, and feasts. It's a fun and interactive way to experience medieval life in the heart of Arizona.
Sedona International Film Festival (February)
 This festival showcases independent films, including documentaries, shorts, and feature films. It's a perfect event for movie enthusiasts and anyone looking to experience the arts in the scenic town of Sedona.

Summer Events

Fourth of July Celebrations

Arizona knows how to throw a Fourth of July party, especially in Flagstaff and Phoenix. You'll find parades, fireworks, and barbecues, making it an excellent time to enjoy the local culture.

Tucson Gem and Mineral Show (February)

For over 60 years, this event has been the largest gem and mineral show in the world. It's a must-visit for anyone interested in jewelry, fossils, and other natural treasures.

Fall Events

Arizona State Fair (October)

Held annually in Phoenix, the Arizona State Fair features carnival rides, games, concerts, and a variety of food vendors. It's a great family-friendly event to enjoy classic fair entertainment.

Scottsdale Culinary Festival (April)

A top culinary event in the state, the Scottsdale Culinary Festival features local chefs, food tastings, and cooking demonstrations. It's a must for food lovers!

Phoenix Lights Festival (November)

This annual music and art festival takes place in Phoenix and attracts thousands of people to celebrate the best in electronic dance music. With over 50 artists and immersive art installations, it's an event for music lovers.

Winter Events

Holiday Lights at the Desert Botanical Garden (December)

A spectacular winter attraction, the Desert Botanical Garden in Phoenix transforms into a wonderland of lights and colorful displays during the holidays. It's a magical experience for all ages.

Winterfest in Flagstaff (December)

Flagstaff's charming downtown area hosts Winterfest, featuring ice skating, holiday lights, and snow-related activities for the whole family. It's perfect for anyone looking to experience a winter wonderland with a cozy, small-town feel.

Arizona's festivals and events provide visitors with unique ways to experience the local culture, cuisine, and arts. Whether you're into outdoor events, food festivals, or cultural celebrations, there's something for everyone, no matter when you visit.

3.4 Planning Around Crowds

Arizona is a popular tourist destination, attracting millions of visitors each year. While the state offers many incredible sites and experiences, some areas can become crowded, particularly during peak travel seasons. To ensure a more enjoyable and stress-free trip, it's important to plan around these crowds. Here's how to navigate busy times and make the most of your visit to the Grand Canyon **State:**

Peak Travel Seasons

Winter (December to February): Winter is a busy season in Arizona, particularly for visitors flocking to cities like Phoenix and Scottsdale, which enjoy mild weather perfect for outdoor activities. The Grand Canyon also attracts tourists who want to experience the snow-capped views. Arizona's ski resorts, such as Arizona Snowbowl near Flagstaff, also see higher traffic during this time. The holidays, from Thanksgiving through New Year's, are especially crowded as many people head to Arizona to escape the colder northern climates.

Spring (March to May): Spring break and the months that follow bring tourists to the state for warm weather and outdoor activities. Popular sites like Sedona and Lake Powell can get particularly crowded, especially during the Tucson Festival of Books or the Arizona Renaissance Festival. Additionally, spring training for major league baseball teams in Phoenix and Scottsdale can draw big crowds, leading to busier-than-usual conditions.

Summer (June to August): Summer in Arizona can be very hot, especially in the desert regions like Phoenix and Yuma, but it's a popular time for families to visit. Visitors head to higher elevations, such as Flagstaff, Sedona, and the Grand Canyon, to escape the heat and enjoy outdoor activities. The crowds can be thick, and hotel prices tend to rise during this time.

Fall (September to November): Fall is one of the best times to visit Arizona, as the temperatures begin to cool, and outdoor activities like hiking, cycling, and sightseeing are at their best. However, popular destinations like Sedona, the Grand Canyon, and Phoenix can get crowded, especially during the weekends and major fall festivals, such as the Arizona State Fair in October.

How to Avoid the Crowds

If you prefer a more relaxed and quieter experience, here are some tips for avoiding the large crowds:

1. Visit During Off-Peak Times

The best times to visit Arizona without the large crowds are typically late fall (October to early November) and early spring (March to early April). These months offer pleasant weather and fewer tourists, especially if you avoid school holidays and spring break. Visiting on weekdays rather than weekends can also make a big difference, particularly at popular spots like the Grand Canyon.

2. Choose Lesser-Known Destinations

While places like the Grand Canyon, Sedona, and Phoenix are iconic and definitely worth visiting, Arizona has many other hidden gems that are less crowded but still offer amazing experiences. Consider exploring areas like:

Payson: A charming town located in the Tonto National Forest, ideal for hiking, camping, and fishing, without the crowds of Sedona.

Tombstone: A historic ghost town that offers an authentic Wild West experience.

Pinetop-Lakeside: A scenic area with lakes, forests, and fewer tourists, perfect for hiking and wildlife watching.

Exploring off-the-beaten-path areas can offer a peaceful experience with fewer crowds.

3. Plan Your Visits Early or Late in the Day

Popular spots like the Grand Canyon and Sedona can be quite crowded during midday, especially during peak seasons. Consider visiting early in the morning or late in the afternoon when most tourists are either just arriving or winding down for the day. The early hours also provide an opportunity to experience cooler temperatures and stunning sunrises, especially at the Grand Canyon.

4. Book Accommodations in Advance

During peak seasons, hotels and resorts in popular areas can fill up quickly, resulting in higher prices and limited availability. Make sure to book your accommodations well in advance to secure a room at your preferred location. This is particularly important for areas like Sedona, the Grand Canyon, and Scottsdale, which see large numbers of visitors.

5. Be Flexible with Your Itinerary

Sometimes, unexpected events like a popular festival, a sports event, or road closures can create crowded conditions at major tourist sites. If you find that a location is too crowded, consider having a backup plan or alternate destinations that are just as enjoyable. For example, if the Grand Canyon is packed, consider taking a scenic drive along Highway 89 or visiting Antelope Canyon instead.

The Benefits of Traveling in Crowds

While avoiding crowds is often ideal for some travelers, there are also benefits to traveling during peak times:

Better Availability of Guided Tours and Activities: During the peak seasons, many attractions and outdoor activities have additional tour options and special events that may only be available at certain times of the year.

Social Atmosphere: Some people enjoy the vibrant social energy that comes with large crowds. Festivals, popular restaurants, and well-known attractions are busier during the peak season, which can offer a more lively experience for travelers who like being in the center of the action.

Key Takeaways

Arizona's peak travel seasons are winter, spring, summer, and fall, with crowds particularly heavy around holidays and major festivals.

To avoid crowds, visit during the shoulder seasons (late fall or early spring), explore lesser-known destinations, and plan visits to popular spots early in the morning or late in the day.

Booking accommodations in advance and being flexible with your itinerary can help reduce stress during peak times.

Whether you prefer the hustle and bustle or a more tranquil experience, planning around the crowds can make your Arizona visit a truly unforgettable one.

Chapter 4: Top Attractions and Destinations

4.1 Grand Canyon National Park

One of the most iconic natural wonders of the world, **Grand Canyon National Park** is a must-see for anyone visiting Arizona. This massive, awe-inspiring canyon stretches over **277 miles (446 kilometers)**, reaching depths of more than **6,000 feet (1,800 meters)**. Whether you're visiting for a day or planning to explore for a few days, the Grand Canyon promises a truly unforgettable experience.

How to Get There

The Grand Canyon is located in northern Arizona, and there are a few ways to get there depending on where you're coming from:

- **By Car**: The most common way to reach the Grand Canyon is by car. If you're driving from **Phoenix**, it takes about **3.5 to 4 hours** (about **230 miles**) to get to the **South Rim**, which is the most popular entrance. If you're coming from **Sedona**, it's around **2 hours** (115 miles). The **North Rim** is less accessible but still worth visiting, especially in the warmer months, and it's about **4.5 hours** from the South Rim.

- **By Air**: The nearest major airport to the Grand Canyon is **Flagstaff Pulliam Airport (FLG)**, which is about **1.5 hours** from the park. Another option is flying into **Phoenix Sky Harbor International Airport (PHX)**, which has more flights and is about a **3.5-hour drive** from the Grand Canyon.

- **Shuttle Service**: From **Phoenix** and **Flagstaff**, shuttle services and guided tours are available. **Grand Canyon Railway** also offers train rides from **Williams, Arizona**, to the South Rim, providing a scenic and unique experience.

What to Do and See at the Grand Canyon

1. South Rim:

The **South Rim** is the most visited part of the park and offers a wide variety of activities, viewpoints, and accommodations. Here's a look at some of the must-see and must-do activities:

- **Scenic Overlooks**: The South Rim is home to several breathtaking viewpoints, including **Mather Point**, **Yaki Point**, and **Hopi Point**. These overlooks offer panoramic views of the canyon's dramatic cliffs, layers of colorful rock, and winding Colorado River below.

- **Grand Canyon Village**: This historic area includes the **El Tovar Hotel**, the **Bright Angel Lodge**, and several museums and visitor centers, including the **Grand Canyon Railway Depot**. The village also serves as the starting point for many of the park's hiking trails.

- **Hiking**: Whether you're looking for an easy stroll or a challenging backcountry hike, the Grand Canyon offers trails for all levels. The **Bright Angel Trail** and **South Kaibab Trail** are two of the most popular and provide access to spectacular canyon views. For those seeking a more immersive experience, a hike to the **Colorado River** at the canyon's bottom is a serious adventure (it takes 1-2 days, so plan accordingly).

- **Ranger Programs**: The park offers a variety of educational programs led by park rangers, including guided hikes, geology talks, and stargazing events.

These programs are free and a great way to learn more about the canyon's history, geology, and wildlife.

- **Sunrise and Sunset Viewing**: The Grand Canyon is famous for its stunning sunrises and sunsets. **Hopi Point** and **Mather Point** are great spots to watch the sun cast golden hues over the canyon's rock formations.

2. North Rim:

The **North Rim** is less crowded and offers a quieter, more remote experience, although it is only open from mid-May to mid-October due to snow in the winter months. Here, you'll find:

- **Bright Angel Point**: This scenic viewpoint offers amazing views of the canyon and is accessible via a short paved trail from the **North Rim Visitor Center**.

- **North Kaibab Trail**: The **North Kaibab Trail** is the only major trail that descends into the canyon from the North Rim. It's less crowded than the South Rim trails but still offers magnificent views.

Things to Know Before You Go

- **Entry Fees**:

  - The entrance fee for Grand Canyon National Park is **$35** per vehicle, which is valid for seven days.
  - You can also buy an annual **America the Beautiful National Parks and Federal Recreational Lands Pass** for $80, which grants access to all U.S. national parks for a year.
- **Open Hours**: The Grand Canyon is open 24 hours a day, year-round, though services (lodging, shuttle buses, etc.) may be limited during the off-season (mid-November through mid-February).

- **Accommodations**: There are a variety of places to stay inside and outside the park, ranging from campgrounds to luxury lodges. The **El Tovar Hotel** and **Bright Angel Lodge** are located on the South Rim and offer historic accommodations with incredible canyon views.

- **Weather Considerations**: The weather can vary greatly depending on the time of year and the location within the park. The **South Rim** is relatively mild in summer but can get cold in winter. The **North Rim** is cooler and can experience snow from October through May. It's essential to check the weather forecast before your trip.

Tips for Visiting the Grand Canyon

- **Plan Ahead**: Due to its popularity, the Grand Canyon can get crowded, especially during summer months and holidays. To avoid the rush, try visiting early in the morning or later in the evening. Weekdays are typically less crowded than weekends.

- **Bring Water**: The Arizona desert can be hot and dry, especially during the summer. Always carry plenty of water, especially if you're hiking.

- **Wear Proper Footwear**: If you plan on hiking, make sure to wear sturdy shoes with good support. The trails are often rocky and uneven, so good footwear is essential.

- **Respect the Park**: The Grand Canyon is a UNESCO World Heritage site, and it's important to follow park rules, stay on designated trails, and avoid disturbing wildlife.

Key Contacts and Information

- **Grand Canyon National Park South Rim**
  Address: Grand Canyon Village, AZ 86023
  Phone: +1 (928) 638-7888 (for general information)
  Website: www.nps.gov/grca

- **Grand Canyon North Rim**
  Address: Grand Canyon, AZ 86052
  Phone: +1 (928) 638-7888 (for North Rim info)

Website: www.nps.gov/grca

Conclusion

The **Grand Canyon National Park** is one of the most remarkable places you can visit in Arizona. Whether you're there to hike, enjoy the views, or simply experience the sheer scale of the canyon, it's an adventure like no other. Make sure to plan your visit ahead of time to fully appreciate everything this natural wonder has to offer!

4.2 Sedona and Red Rock Country

Nestled in the heart of Arizona's Verde Valley, Sedona and its surrounding Red Rock Country are famous for their breathtaking landscapes, vibrant arts scene, and spiritual allure. Known for its iconic red sandstone formations, this stunning destination draws visitors from around the world to explore its natural beauty, enjoy outdoor adventures, and experience a sense of tranquility. Whether you're looking to hike, meditate, or simply take in the views, Sedona offers something for everyone.

Red Rock Scenic Byway (SR 179): This scenic drive takes you past some of Sedona's most famous formations, including Bell Rock and Courthouse Butte. It's one of the best ways to enjoy the striking red landscape without venturing far off the beaten path.

Oak Creek Canyon Drive: This winding road offers stunning views of the canyon and is especially beautiful during the fall when the foliage turns vibrant colors. You can also stop for a peaceful picnic along the creek.

3. Vortex Sites:

Sedona is known for its powerful vortex sites, areas believed to have strong spiritual energy that can promote healing and relaxation. These sites attract people interested in meditation, yoga, and spiritual exploration. Some of the best-known vortex sites include:

Airport Mesa: Known for its stunning 360-degree views, Airport Mesa is a popular spot for both vortex energy and sunset viewing.

Bell Rock: Bell Rock is one of the most powerful vortex sites and is popular for meditation and spiritual reflection.

Boynton Canyon: Another strong vortex site, Boynton Canyon offers peaceful hiking trails, beautiful views, and a serene atmosphere ideal for quiet reflection.

4. Sedona Arts and Culture:

Sedona is a hub for creativity, with an impressive arts scene that includes galleries, art festivals, and cultural events. Whether you're into fine art, photography, or pottery, Sedona's artistic atmosphere offers plenty to explore:

Tlaquepaque Arts & Crafts Village: This charming outdoor shopping center features galleries, shops, and restaurants in a beautiful setting. Tlaquepaque is home to a wide variety of local artisans, and you'll find everything from paintings to jewelry and pottery.

Sedona Arts Center: Established in 1958, this nonprofit arts center hosts workshops, exhibits, and performances. It's a great place to take an art class or view work by local artists.

Annual Events: Sedona is known for its art festivals, including the Sedona Arts Festival and the Red Rock Fantasy light display. These events are perfect for immersing yourself in the community's vibrant arts culture.

5. Relaxation and Wellness:

Sedona is also known as a wellness destination, attracting visitors who are looking to relax and recharge in a serene environment. The area offers a variety of spas and wellness retreats, many of which take advantage of the peaceful desert setting and the spiritual energy of the vortex sites.

Spa Resorts: There are a number of luxurious spas and resorts in Sedona offering everything from massages to yoga retreats. Popular choices include the L'Auberge de Sedona and Enchantment Resort, both of which offer stunning views and **top-notch wellness experiences**.

Wellness Centers: Sedona is home to many wellness centers that focus on holistic treatments like Reiki, energy healing, and sound therapy. You can schedule a private session to unwind or participate in group meditation and yoga.

Things to Know Before You Go

Weather Considerations: Sedona enjoys a mild climate, making it a great year-round destination. However, summers can be hot, with temperatures reaching into the 90s°F (30s°C), so be sure to pack sunscreen, a hat, and plenty of water. Winters are cooler but still mild, with temperatures averaging between 40-60°F (4-15°C).

Entry Fees: Many of Sedona's outdoor activities, such as hiking and scenic drives, are free. However, some areas, like Slide Rock State Park, charge an entry fee (about $20 per vehicle).

Accommodations: There's a wide range of places to stay in Sedona, from luxury resorts to charming bed-and-breakfasts. Popular spots include the L'Auberge de Sedona, Enchantment Resort, and the Sedona Rouge Hotel.

Key Contacts and Information

Sedona Chamber of Commerce & Visitor Center
 Address: 331 Forest Road, Sedona, AZ 86336
 Phone: +1 (928) 282-7722
 Website: www.visitsedona.com

Slide Rock State Park
 Address: 6871 N. Hwy 89A, Sedona, AZ 86336
 Phone: +1 (928) 282-3034
 Website: www.azstateparks.com/slide-rock

Conclusion

Sedona and Red Rock Country offer some of the most stunning scenery and unique experiences in Arizona. Whether you're hiking through the red rock canyons, exploring the local arts scene, or simply relaxing at a wellness retreat, Sedona is the perfect destination for those seeking natural beauty and inner peace. The beauty of the landscape, combined with the energy of the vortex sites, makes Sedona a truly magical place to visit.

4.3 Phoenix and the Valley of the Sun

The Valley of the Sun, which encompasses Phoenix and its surrounding cities, is the heart of Arizona and one of the most vibrant urban areas in the American Southwest. Phoenix, Arizona's capital, is known for its modern cityscape, rich history, and striking desert surroundings. The area offers a blend of outdoor activities, cultural experiences, and world-class dining and entertainment. Whether you're looking to explore the desert landscapes, visit historical sites, or enjoy a bustling metropolitan area, Phoenix and the Valley of the Sun have something to offer every type of traveler.

How to Get There

Phoenix is easily accessible by car, air, and public transportation.

By Car: Phoenix is centrally located in Arizona, making it a key starting point for most road trips in the state. It's well connected via major highways like I-10, I-17, and Loop 101. It's about 4 hours from Sedona and 6 hours from Flagstaff by car.

By Air: The primary airport for Phoenix is Phoenix Sky Harbor International Airport (PHX), located just 5 miles east of downtown Phoenix. It's one of the busiest airports in the country and offers direct flights from across the U.S. and abroad.

By Public Transport: Phoenix is served by Greyhound and Megabus for long-distance travel, with buses connecting to other major cities in Arizona and beyond. Valley Metro also offers bus services within the city, and there's a light rail system connecting Phoenix to surrounding cities like Tempe and Mesa.

What to Do and See in Phoenix

Phoenix is a sprawling city with diverse attractions. From outdoor adventures to cultural and historical sites, you'll find plenty to keep you busy:

1. Desert Botanical Garden:
The Desert Botanical Garden is a must-see for anyone visiting Phoenix. Situated in Papago Park, the garden spans 140 acres and showcases more than 50,000 plants, including many native desert species. It's a peaceful place to learn about the desert's unique ecosystems and is a perfect spot for a relaxing stroll.
Entry Fee: Around $25 for adults (prices may vary with special events).
Hours: Daily from 7:00 AM – 8:00 PM (check for seasonal changes).
Address: 1201 N. Galvin Parkway, Phoenix, AZ 85008
Phone: +1 (480) 941-1225
Website: www.dbg.org

2. Heard Museum:
If you're interested in learning about Native American culture, the Heard Museum is an excellent stop. It's home to an impressive collection of Native American art and artifacts, with exhibits that explore the history, culture, and art of Indigenous peoples from across the Americas. The museum's Arizona history exhibit is particularly insightful for understanding the region's heritage.
Entry Fee: Around $20 for adults.
Hours: Monday to Saturday, 9:30 AM – 5:00 PM; Sunday 11:00 AM – 5:00 PM.

Address: 2301 N. Central Avenue, Phoenix, AZ 85004
Phone: +1 (602) 252-8840
Website: www.heard.org

3. Desert Ridge Marketplace and Entertainment District:
For a more modern experience, visit the Desert Ridge Marketplace in North Phoenix. This open-air shopping and entertainment complex is home to retail stores, restaurants, and entertainment venues like the AMC Desert Ridge 18 cinema and live music at various venues. It's a great place for shopping and enjoying some live entertainment.
Hours: Varies by store and restaurant (typically 10:00 AM – 9:00 PM).
Address: 21001 N. Tatum Blvd., Phoenix, AZ 85050
Phone: +1 (602) 765-5550
Website: www.desertridge.com

4. Camelback Mountain:
For outdoor enthusiasts, Camelback Mountain is one of the most popular hikes in Phoenix. The mountain gets its name from the rock formations that resemble a camel's back. There are two main trails to the summit, the Echo Canyon Trail (more challenging) and the Cholla Trail (a bit easier but still strenuous). The summit provides amazing views of the city below and the surrounding desert landscape.
Entry Fee: Free to hike; parking can be difficult to find, and there are no official entry fees, though parking lots may charge.
Hours: Open daily, but it's best to hike early in the morning or in the cooler months (October – April).
Address: 6135 E. Cholla Lane, Phoenix, AZ 85018
Phone: +1 (602) 262-7901 (City of Phoenix Parks and Recreation)
Website: www.phoenix.gov/parks

5. Old Town Scottsdale:
Just a short drive from Phoenix, Old Town Scottsdale offers a more laid-back vibe, with its charming historic district full of Southwestern-style shops, art galleries, and restaurants. The area is perfect for a leisurely stroll, browsing for souvenirs, or enjoying a meal at one of the local eateries.

Hours: Varies by store and restaurant (generally 10:00 AM – 9:00 PM).
Address: Main Street, Scottsdale, AZ 85251
Phone: +1 (480) 312-7750 (Scottsdale Visitor Center)
Website: www.oldtownscottsdale.com

6. Heard Museum and Art Walk:

Phoenix is also known for its vibrant arts scene. The First Fridays Art Walk (held on the first Friday of every month) is a popular event where galleries throughout downtown Phoenix open their doors to the public for special exhibits, live music, and performances. It's a fun way to explore Phoenix's creative side.

Things to Know Before You Go

Weather Considerations: Phoenix experiences a desert climate, so expect hot summers with temperatures reaching over 100°F (38°C). Winters are mild, with daytime highs around 60-70°F (15-21°C). Be sure to bring sunscreen, a hat, and plenty of water, especially if you plan on hiking.

Entry Fees: Some attractions, such as the Desert Botanical Garden and Heard Museum, have entry fees (typically around $20 for adults). Always check for discounts or special event pricing.

Accommodations: Phoenix offers a wide range of accommodations, from luxury resorts like The Phoenician to more budget-friendly options. Popular areas to stay include Downtown Phoenix, Scottsdale, and Tempe.

Key Contacts and Information

Phoenix Visitor Information Center
 Address: 100 W. Washington Street, Phoenix, AZ 85003
 Phone: +1 (602) 254-6500
 Website: www.visitphoenix.com

Desert Botanical Garden
 Address: 1201 N. Galvin Parkway, Phoenix, AZ 85008
 Phone: +1 (480) 941-1225
 Website: www.dbg.org

Conclusion

Phoenix and the Valley of the Sun offer a perfect blend of desert adventure, cultural discovery, and urban excitement. Whether you're hiking up Camelback Mountain, enjoying the arts in Scottsdale, or exploring the Heard Museum, you'll find something for every interest and age group. With its sunny weather, beautiful desert landscapes, and rich cultural history, Phoenix is a must-visit destination for anyone traveling through Arizona.

4.4 Tucson and Southern Arizona

Tucson, nestled in the heart of Southern Arizona, offers a captivating blend of history, culture, and breathtaking desert landscapes. Known as the "Old Pueblo," Tucson is a vibrant city surrounded by majestic mountains and the sprawling Sonoran Desert. This region boasts a rich Native American and Mexican heritage, celebrated through its cuisine, festivals, and historical landmarks. Southern Arizona is a haven for nature enthusiasts, history buffs, and food lovers alike.

How to Get to Tucson

By Air: Tucson International Airport (TUS) is about 8 miles from downtown and offers flights from major U.S. cities. Shuttle services and car rentals are readily available at the airport.

By Car: Tucson is easily accessible via Interstate 10, approximately a 2-hour drive from Phoenix.

By Train: Amtrak's Sunset Limited and Texas Eagle routes stop in Tucson, connecting it to cities like Los Angeles and New Orleans.

By Bus: Greyhound and FlixBus provide services to Tucson from various cities.

What to Do and See in Tucson and Southern Arizona

1. Saguaro National Park

Tucson is home to the iconic Saguaro National Park, which showcases the stunning beauty of the Sonoran Desert. Split into two districts—East (Rincon Mountain District) and West (Tucson Mountain District)—the park offers hiking, scenic drives, and plenty of opportunities to photograph the towering saguaro cacti.

Entry Fee: $25 per vehicle (valid for 7 days).

Hours: Open daily from sunrise to sunset. Visitor centers are open from 9:00 AM to 5:00 PM.

Address: Multiple entry points—check the website for details.

Contact: +1 (520) 733-5153 | www.nps.gov/sagu

2. Arizona-Sonora Desert Museum

This world-renowned museum is part zoo, botanical garden, and natural history museum, offering a comprehensive look at the flora and fauna of the Sonoran Desert. Highlights include live animal exhibits, an aviary, and desert-inspired art galleries.

Entry Fee: Around $25 for adults, $15 for children.

Hours: Daily from 7:30 AM to 5:00 PM.

Address: 2021 N. Kinney Road, Tucson, AZ 85743.

Contact: +1 (520) 883-2702 | www.desertmuseum.org

3. Mission San Xavier del Bac

This beautifully preserved Spanish mission, often called the "White Dove of the

Desert," is a must-see for history enthusiasts. Built in the late 1700s, it remains an active Catholic church and a masterpiece of Baroque architecture.

Entry Fee: Free (donations encouraged).

Hours: Daily from 8:00 AM to 5:00 PM.

Address: 1950 W. San Xavier Road, Tucson, AZ 85746.

Contact: +1 (520) 294-2624 | www.sanxaviermission.org

4. University of Arizona and Downtown Tucson

Explore the vibrant culture of Tucson at the University of Arizona, which houses attractions like the Arizona State Museum and the Flandrau Science Center and Planetarium. Stroll through Downtown Tucson for unique shops, art galleries, and excellent dining options, including authentic Mexican food.

Key Events:

Tucson Gem and Mineral Show (held annually in February).

Tucson Meet Yourself Festival (celebrates the city's cultural diversity).

5. Tombstone and Bisbee

Take a short drive from Tucson to explore the historic towns of Tombstone and Bisbee. Tombstone, known for the legendary Gunfight at the O.K. Corral, offers reenactments, museums, and Old West saloons. Bisbee is a charming mining town with an artistic flair, featuring unique galleries and the famous Queen Mine Tour.

Tombstone Entry Fee: Most attractions have individual fees; O.K. Corral admission is around $10.

Bisbee Queen Mine Tour: $13 for adults.

Where to Eat in Tucson

1. El Charro Café

Founded in 1922, this iconic restaurant claims to be the birthplace of the chimichanga. Enjoy classic Mexican dishes made with fresh, local ingredients.

Price: $10–$25 per meal.

Address: Multiple locations in Tucson.

Contact: +1 (520) 622-1922 | www.elcharrocafe.com

2. Barrio Bread

Known for its artisan bread and local ingredients, Barrio Bread is a favorite among locals and visitors.

Price: $5–$15.

Address: 18 S. Eastbourne Avenue, Tucson, AZ 85716.

Contact: +1 (520) 327-1292 | www.barriobread.com

Things to Know Before Visiting Tucson

Weather: Summers are hot, with temperatures exceeding 100°F (38°C). Winters are mild and ideal for outdoor activities, with highs around 65°F (18°C).

Accommodations: Options range from luxury resorts like the Loews Ventana Canyon Resort to charming bed-and-breakfasts. Prices vary from $100–$400 per night depending on the season.

Packing Tips: Sunscreen, sunglasses, and sturdy hiking shoes are essential. If visiting in winter, bring layers for cooler evenings.

Key Contacts for Visitors

Visit Tucson:

 Address: 100 S. Church Avenue, Tucson, AZ 85701.

 Phone: +1 (520) 624-1817.

 Website: www.visittucson.org

Tucson and Southern Arizona offer a perfect mix of natural beauty, rich history, and cultural vibrancy. From exploring the towering saguaros in the desert to walking the historic streets of Tombstone, this region promises an unforgettable journey into the heart of the Southwest.

4.5 Monument Valley and the Navajo Nation

Monument Valley is one of the most iconic landscapes in the American Southwest, instantly recognizable from countless films, photographs, and postcards. Located within the Navajo Nation, this majestic area is characterized by towering sandstone buttes, vast desert plains, and a rich cultural heritage. Visiting Monument Valley offers an incredible opportunity to connect with the land, learn about Navajo traditions, and experience some of the most stunning vistas in the United States.

How to Get to Monument Valley
By Car:
 Monument Valley is located near the Arizona-Utah border, about a 4-hour drive from Flagstaff, Arizona, and a 2.5-hour drive from Page, Arizona. From Flagstaff, take US-89 north, then US-160 east, and finally US-163 north.
By Air:
 The closest major airports are Flagstaff Pulliam Airport (FLG) and Page Municipal Airport (PGA). Rental cars are essential for reaching the area.
By Tour:
 Guided tours are available from cities like Flagstaff, Sedona, and Phoenix, providing transportation and curated experiences.
What to Do and See at Monument Valley
1. Monument Valley Tribal Park
 Managed by the Navajo Nation, this park is the heart of Monument Valley and a must-visit destination. Highlights include iconic formations such as The Mittens, Totem Pole, and John Ford's Point.
Entry Fee: $8 per person (subject to change).
Hours: Daily from 6:00 AM to 8:00 PM (seasonal variations).
Address: US-163 Scenic, Oljato-Monument Valley, AZ 84536.

Contact: +1 (435) 727-5870 | www.navajonationparks.org

2. Scenic Drive
 Take the 17-mile Valley Drive, a dirt road that winds through some of the most famous landmarks. You can self-drive or join a guided tour led by Navajo guides who share stories, legends, and cultural insights.
Guided Tour Price: $75–$100 per person for a group tour; private tours may cost more.
Tips: High-clearance vehicles are recommended for self-driving due to rough terrain.

3. Guided Tours and Cultural Experiences
 Explore Monument Valley through a Navajo-guided tour, which often includes access to restricted areas, visits to ancient petroglyphs, and storytelling around sacred sites. Some tours even offer a traditional Navajo meal or a chance to attend a cultural performance.

Popular Tour Providers: Navajo Spirit Tours, Monument Valley Safari.
Contact: Prices range from $80–$150 depending on the tour length and type.
4. Goulding's Lodge and Museum
 Goulding's Lodge is a historic spot that served as a hub for filmmakers during the golden age of Western movies. Today, it features a museum showcasing Monument Valley's role in Hollywood, a gift shop, and stunning views of the valley.
Entry Fee (Museum): $10 per person.
Hours: Daily from 9:00 AM to 6:00 PM.
Address: 1000 Gouldings Trading Post Road, Monument Valley, UT 84536.
Contact: +1 (435) 727-3231 | www.gouldings.com
Where to Stay Near Monument Valley
1. The View Hotel
 The only hotel located within Monument Valley Tribal Park, offering unparalleled views of the formations right from your balcony.
Price: $250–$450 per night depending on the season.
Address: Indian Route 42, Oljato-Monument Valley, AZ 84536.
Contact: +1 (435) 727-5555 | www.monumentvalleyview.com

2. Goulding's Lodge

A historic lodge with comfortable accommodations, RV spots, and guided tour services.
Price: $200–$350 per night.
Contact: +1 (435) 727-3231.

3. Camping

Monument Valley KOA Journey offers a convenient camping option with modern amenities.
Price: $30–$60 per night.

Cultural Etiquette and Tips

Respect the Land: Monument Valley is sacred to the Navajo people. Stay on designated trails, avoid touching rock formations, and respect restricted areas.
Photography: Always ask for permission before photographing Navajo people or cultural sites.
Cultural Awareness: Consider participating in Navajo-led tours to gain a deeper understanding of their traditions and history.

Packing Tips

Sunscreen, sunglasses, and plenty of water are essential, as the desert sun can be intense.
Bring sturdy shoes for hiking and exploring.
Layered clothing is recommended; temperatures can vary significantly between day and night.
Key Contacts for Visitors
Monument Valley Tribal Park Office: +1 (435) 727-5870.
Navajo Nation Tourism: www.discovernavajo.com.
Monument Valley and the Navajo Nation offer more than just stunning landscapes—they provide a journey into a world rich with culture, history, and natural wonder. Whether you're exploring towering buttes, learning about Navajo traditions, or simply marveling at the vast desert vistas, this is a destination that promises unforgettable memories.

4.6 Saguaro National Park and the Desert Landscape

Saguaro National Park, located near Tucson, Arizona, is a striking tribute to the beauty and resilience of the Sonoran Desert. Named after the iconic saguaro cactus, this park showcases diverse desert flora and fauna, breathtaking landscapes, and unique ecosystems that highlight the beauty of Arizona's arid wilderness.

Divided into two districts—the Tucson Mountain District (West) and the Rincon Mountain District (East)—Saguaro National Park offers visitors endless opportunities to explore the natural wonders of the desert.

How to Get to Saguaro National Park
By Car:
The Tucson Mountain District (West) is about 15 miles west of downtown Tucson. Take Speedway Boulevard west to Gates Pass Road.
The Rincon Mountain District (East) is approximately 10 miles east of Tucson. Use Broadway Boulevard to Old Spanish Trail.
By Air:
 Tucson International Airport (TUS) is the nearest major airport, located about 30 minutes from either district.

What to Do and See at Saguaro National Park
1. Scenic Drives
Cactus Forest Drive (Rincon Mountain District): A 8-mile paved loop that offers stunning views of saguaro forests and desert scenery.
Bajada Loop Drive (Tucson Mountain District): A 5-mile unpaved loop that provides access to some of the park's most picturesque trails.
Tip: Both drives have pullouts for photography and short walks.

2. Hiking Trails

Saguaro National Park has over 165 miles of trails, ranging from easy nature walks to challenging hikes.

Signal Hill Trail (West): A short 0.8-mile hike featuring ancient petroglyphs.

Freeman Homestead Trail (East): A 1.1-mile loop with interpretive signs about desert life.

Esperero Trail (West): A more strenuous hike for seasoned adventurers with rewarding views.

3. Saguaro Cactus Viewing

The park is home to one of the most extensive concentrations of saguaro cacti, some of which are over 150 years old and stand more than 40 feet tall. Visit during spring to see the cacti bloom with white flowers, Arizona's state flower.

4. Ranger-Led Programs

Engage in guided hikes, stargazing events, and educational talks led by park rangers. These programs are designed to deepen your understanding of desert ecosystems and the cultural significance of the area.

Cost: Most programs are free with park admission.

Availability: Check the park's website for a current schedule.

5. Visitor Centers

Each district has a visitor center with exhibits, maps, and knowledgeable staff.

Tucson Mountain Visitor Center (West): Features displays about the Sonoran Desert.

Rincon Mountain Visitor Center (East): Offers insight into the park's geology and wildlife.

Hours: Open daily from 9:00 AM to 5:00 PM.

Park Fees and Hours

Entrance Fee: $25 per vehicle, $15 per person (hiking or biking), valid for seven days.

Annual Pass: $45, granting unlimited access to Saguaro National Park for a year.

Hours: The park is open year-round from sunrise to sunset. Visitor center hours may vary.

Where to Stay Near Saguaro National Park

1. Tucson Resorts and Hotels

JW Marriott Tucson Starr Pass Resort: Luxury accommodations with desert views.

Price: $250–$400 per night.

Contact: +1 (520) 792-3500.

Hacienda Del Sol Guest Ranch Resort: A historic boutique hotel.

Price: $200–$350 per night.

2. Camping Options

 While camping is not permitted within the park, nearby sites include:

Gilbert Ray Campground: Located in Tucson Mountain Park, just outside the park's west boundary.

Price: $20 per night for tent sites.

Wildlife and Desert Ecosystem

Saguaro National Park is home to a diverse range of desert wildlife:

Mammals: Coyotes, javelinas, bobcats.

Birds: Cactus wrens, roadrunners, and Gambel's quail.

Reptiles: Gila monsters, desert tortoises, and various lizards.

Pro Tip: Wildlife is most active during early morning or evening hours. Always maintain a safe distance.

Tips for Visiting

Hydration: Bring plenty of water, especially during the warmer months.

Sun Protection: Use sunscreen, sunglasses, and a wide-brimmed hat.

Best Time to Visit: Late fall, winter, and early spring offer cooler temperatures ideal for hiking.

Safety: Be cautious of rattlesnakes and avoid wandering off marked trails.

Contact Information

Address:

 Tucson Mountain District: 2700 N Kinney Rd, Tucson, AZ 85743.

 Rincon Mountain District: 3693 S Old Spanish Trail, Tucson, AZ 85730.

Phone: +1 (520) 733-5153.

Website: www.nps.gov/sagu

Saguaro National Park offers a captivating glimpse into Arizona's desert beauty and cultural heritage. Whether you're marveling at the towering cacti, hiking scenic trails, or enjoying a quiet sunset over the desert, this park is a must-see destination that embodies the heart of the Southwest.

4.7 Hoover Dam and Lake Mead

The Hoover Dam and Lake Mead stand as testaments to engineering ingenuity and natural beauty. Though Hoover Dam straddles the border of Arizona and Nevada, its proximity makes it a must-visit destination for anyone exploring Arizona. The dam, completed in 1935, was a marvel of its time, taming the mighty Colorado River to provide water and hydroelectric power to the Southwest. Nearby, Lake Mead, the reservoir formed by the dam, offers an array of recreational activities, making this area a blend of history, innovation, and outdoor fun.

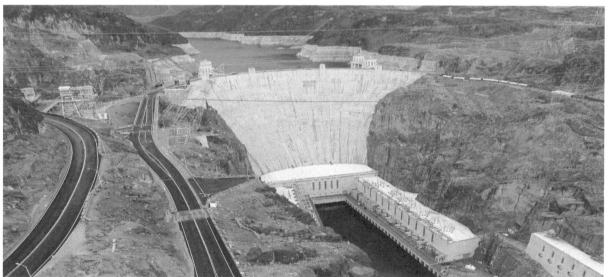

How to Get to Hoover Dam and Lake Mead

By Car:

From Phoenix: It's about a 4.5-hour drive (approx. 250 miles). Take I-17 North to I-40 West, then U.S. Route 93 North.

From Las Vegas: Hoover Dam is about a 45-minute drive (approx. 35 miles) southeast via U.S. Route 93.

By Bus or Tour:

Several guided tours operate from Las Vegas and Phoenix, offering transport and insightful narratives about the dam's history.

Hoover Dam Highlights

1. Visitor Center

The Hoover Dam Visitor Center offers interactive exhibits, historical displays, and a look at the dam's inner workings.

Admission Fee: $10 for the Visitor Center only; $30 for the full Powerplant Tour.

Hours: Open daily from 9:00 AM to 5:00 PM.

2. Guided Tours

Explore the dam's inner workings through guided tours, including a walk through the power plant and a peek into the massive tunnels.

Duration: 30–60 minutes, depending on the tour.

3. Observation Deck
Enjoy panoramic views of the dam, Lake Mead, and the Colorado River. Don't miss the Hoover Dam Bypass Bridge, which offers incredible photo opportunities.

Lake Mead Recreation

1. Boating and Water Sports
Lake Mead is one of the largest man-made reservoirs in the U.S., ideal for boating, jet skiing, and paddleboarding.

Boat Rentals:

Pontoon boats: $300–$500/day.

Jet skis: $150–$250/day.

Available at Lake Mead Marina and Callville Bay Resort.

2. Fishing
Lake Mead is home to striped bass, catfish, and rainbow trout.

Fishing License: Required for all anglers; $55 for a non-resident daily license (includes Nevada and Arizona waters).

3. Hiking and Scenic Views
The Historic Railroad Trail is a 7.5-mile round-trip hike offering views of Lake Mead and the dam. It's family-friendly and follows old railroad tunnels used during the dam's construction.

Hoover Dam History and Legacy
Construction of Hoover Dam began during the Great Depression, employing thousands of workers and transforming the Southwest. The dam, standing 726 feet tall, was the world's tallest concrete dam at the time of its completion. It created Lake Mead, which provides water to over 20 million people across the region.

Fun Fact: The dam was initially called Boulder Dam but was later renamed after President Herbert Hoover in 1947.

Tips for Visiting

Best Time to Visit:
Visit in fall, winter, or spring to avoid extreme summer heat, which can reach over 110°F (43°C).

What to Bring:
Water, especially during the warmer months.
Comfortable walking shoes for exploring the dam and trails.
Sunscreen and hats for outdoor activities.
Security Check:
 Be prepared for security screenings before entering the dam area. Large bags and certain items may be restricted.

Dining and Nearby Accommodations
1. Hoover Dam Lodge
Description: A rustic hotel located just 5 miles from the dam. Offers dining, a casino, and views of Lake Mead.
Price: $150–$250 per night.
Contact: +1 (702) 293-5000.

2. Boulder City
 A charming town near the dam, Boulder City offers dining options like The Coffee Cup Café (known for hearty breakfasts) and Southwest Diner.
Park Fees and Hours
Lake Mead National Recreation Area Entrance Fee:
$25 per vehicle, valid for seven days.
Annual passes available for $45.
Hours:
Hoover Dam: Daily from 9:00 AM to 5:00 PM.
Lake Mead: Open 24/7 for recreational activities.

Contact Information
Hoover Dam Visitor Center: +1 (702) 494-2517.
Lake Mead National Recreation Area: +1 (702) 293-8990.
Website: www.usbr.gov/lc/hooverdam
The Hoover Dam and Lake Mead offer a fascinating mix of history, engineering, and outdoor adventure. Whether marveling at the dam's scale, enjoying water activities on Lake Mead, or hiking the scenic trails, this destination is an unforgettable part of any Arizona travel experience.

Chapter 5: Outdoor Adventures and Activities

5.1 Hiking Trails and Nature Walks

Arizona offers outdoor enthusiasts a wealth of hiking trails and nature walks, showcasing its stunning landscapes from deserts to mountains. With paths suited to all skill levels, this chapter guides you through the best routes, tips, and what to expect on your Arizona adventure.

Top Hiking Trails in Arizona

1. Bright Angel Trail (Grand Canyon National Park)

Overview: A historic and challenging trail descending into the Grand Canyon.

Distance: Up to 12 miles round trip (shorter hikes are possible).

Difficulty: Moderate to strenuous.

Highlights: Breathtaking canyon views, resting spots at Indian Garden, and overnight stays at Phantom Ranch.

Fees: Included in the park entrance fee ($35 per vehicle).

Contact: Grand Canyon National Park Visitor Center, +1 (928) 638-7888.

2. Cathedral Rock Trail (Sedona)

Overview: A steep climb to Sedona's iconic Cathedral Rock.

Distance: 1.2 miles round trip.

Difficulty: Moderate to strenuous.

Highlights: Panoramic views of Sedona's red rock formations, especially during sunset.

Fees: Red Rock Pass required ($5/day).

3. Devil's Bridge Trail (Sedona)

Overview: A popular trail leading to Arizona's largest natural sandstone arch.

Distance: 4.2 miles round trip.

Difficulty: Moderate.

Highlights: The chance to walk across the arch for incredible photos.

Tips: Arrive early as parking fills quickly.

Fees: Free but parking fees may apply.

4. Havasu Falls Trail (Havasupai Reservation)

Overview: A challenging hike leading to turquoise waterfalls in a remote canyon.

Distance: 10 miles one way.

Difficulty: Strenuous.

Permits: Required and must be booked months in advance (~$375/person).

Contact: Havasupai Tribe Tourism Office, +1 (928) 448-2121.

5. Echo Canyon Trail (Camelback Mountain, Phoenix)

Overview: A steep climb up one of Phoenix's most famous peaks.

Distance: 2.4 miles round trip.

Difficulty: Strenuous.

Highlights: Panoramic city views.

Tips: Start early to avoid heat and crowds.

Best Nature Walks for Families

1. Desert Botanical Garden (Phoenix)

Overview: A family-friendly space highlighting Arizona's desert plants.

Distance: Multiple short loops under 1 mile.

Difficulty: Easy.

Highlights: Seasonal exhibits, butterfly pavilion, and nighttime light displays.

Hours: Daily, 8:00 AM–8:00 PM.

Fees: Adults $24.95, children $14.95.

Contact: +1 (480) 941-1225.

2. Watson Lake Loop Trail (Prescott)

Overview: A scenic trail surrounding a beautiful lake.

Distance: 4.8 miles.

Difficulty: Easy to moderate.

Highlights: Granite boulders, water activities, and picnic spots.

Tips: Perfect for families with kids.

Hiking Tips and Safety

Plan Ahead: Research your trail, check the weather, and inform someone of your plans.

Hydrate: Carry at least 1 liter of water per hour of hiking.

Dress Appropriately: Wear comfortable hiking shoes, a wide-brimmed hat, and sunscreen.

Start Early: Avoid the midday heat, especially during summer months.

Respect Nature: Stay on designated trails and follow Leave No Trace principles.

When to Hike in Arizona

Spring (March–May): Ideal temperatures and blooming wildflowers.

Fall (September–November): Cooler weather and smaller crowds.

Winter (December–February): Great for desert trails; some mountain trails may be snow-covered.

Summer (June–August): Stick to early morning hikes or higher elevations to avoid extreme heat.

From iconic trails like Bright Angel in the Grand Canyon to serene family walks in the Desert Botanical Garden, Arizona's hiking and nature experiences promise memories to last a lifetime. Whether you're scaling Camelback Mountain or marveling at the beauty of Sedona's red rocks, adventure awaits around every corner.

5.2 River Rafting and Water Sports

Arizona offers thrilling water-based activities, from adrenaline-pumping river rafting to relaxing water sports in its lakes and rivers. With options ranging from half-day excursions to multi-day adventures, this chapter dives into everything you need to know.

River Rafting Adventures

1. Colorado River (Grand Canyon)

Overview: One of the most iconic river rafting experiences in the world.

Activities: Whitewater rafting, kayaking, and scenic float trips.

Trip Options:

Full Canyon Rafting: 7–14 days ($3,000–$6,000).

Half Canyon Rafting: 4–8 days ($2,000–$4,000).
Day Trips: From $150 per person.
Season: Best between May and September.
Permits: Required for self-guided trips; commercial tours available.
Contact: Grand Canyon National Park, +1 (928) 638-7888.

2. Salt River (Tonto National Forest)
Overview: A popular rafting destination with Class III-IV rapids.
Trip Options: Half-day, full-day, and multi-day trips ($50–$500).
Season: March through May (dependent on snowmelt).
Highlights: Dramatic canyons, wildlife spotting, and lush vegetation.

3. Verde River
Overview: A gentle river ideal for kayaking and paddleboarding.
Difficulty: Easy to moderate.
Season: Year-round.
Highlights: Peaceful floats, bird watching, and historical ruins along the way.
Lakes and Water Sports

1. Lake Powell
Overview: A massive reservoir perfect for boating, jet skiing, and fishing.
Activities:
Houseboat rentals ($1,500–$5,000 per week).
Jet skiing ($200–$400 per day).
Paddleboarding and kayaking ($50–$150 per day).
Access Points: Wahweap Marina and Antelope Point Marina.
Contact: +1 (928) 645-2433.

2. Lake Havasu
Overview: Known for its crystal-clear waters and London Bridge.
Activities: Water skiing, parasailing, and beach lounging.
Season: Popular in spring and summer.
Fees: State park entry $10–$15.
Contact: Lake Havasu Visitor Center, +1 (928) 453-3444.

3. Roosevelt Lake

Overview: A tranquil lake for fishing and boating.
Activities: Bass fishing tournaments, pontoon rentals, and camping.
Highlights: Scenic views of the Superstition Mountains.

Tips for Water Adventures
Check the Weather: Avoid trips during storms or extreme heat.
Safety Gear: Always wear a life jacket and bring a whistle.
Pack Essentials: Sunscreen, water bottles, and waterproof bags are must-haves.
Permits: Verify if a permit is needed for your activity.
Book Early: Popular activities and tours fill up quickly, especially during peak season.

5.3 Desert Exploration and Jeep Tours

Arizona's deserts are brimming with natural wonders, from towering saguaros to mysterious rock formations. Jeep tours and guided excursions make it easy to explore these breathtaking landscapes.

Popular Jeep Tour Destinations
1. Sedona
Overview: Famous for its red rock landscapes and vortex sites.
Tours Offered:
Broken Arrow Trail: Off-road adventure with stunning views ($130–$150 per person).
Scenic Vortex Tours: Visit Sedona's mystical energy centers ($100–$125 per person).
Contact: Pink Jeep Tours Sedona, +1 (800) 873-3662.

2. Sonoran Desert (Scottsdale and Phoenix)
Overview: A rugged landscape filled with unique flora and fauna.
Tours Offered:
Desert Eco Tours: Learn about native plants and animals ($90–$120 per person).
Sunset Jeep Tours: Perfect for photography enthusiasts.

3. Monument Valley
Overview: A striking desert region with iconic sandstone formations.
Tours Offered:

Guided Navajo Jeep Tours: Explore areas inaccessible to the public ($75–$100 per person).

Cultural Tours: Learn about Navajo traditions and history.

4. Superstition Mountains

Overview: A region rich in legends and rugged beauty.

Activities:

Jeep tours to the Lost Dutchman State Park.

Guided hikes to ancient petroglyph sites.

Desert Exploration Tips

Dress for the Desert: Wear light, breathable clothing and sturdy shoes.

Stay Hydrated: Bring more water than you think you'll need.

Protect Yourself: Sunscreen, sunglasses, and a wide-brimmed hat are essential.

Respect the Environment: Do not disturb wildlife or remove plants.

Hire a Guide: Local experts can enhance your experience with insider knowledge and ensure your safety.

From the thrill of river rafting through the Grand Canyon to the serene beauty of Lake Powell and the adventurous allure of jeep tours, Arizona's outdoor adventures offer unforgettable experiences for every traveler. Whether you're paddling down the Salt River or exploring Sedona's rugged trails, there's always a new discovery waiting in the Grand Canyon State.

5.4 Scenic Drives: Route 66 and Beyond

Arizona is a haven for scenic drives, offering breathtaking views, historical landmarks, and unique roadside attractions. Whether you're cruising along the iconic Route 66 or exploring lesser-known highways, there's no shortage of unforgettable journeys.

Route 66: The Mother Road

Overview: Stretching through Northern Arizona, Route 66 passes through charming towns, quirky attractions, and stunning landscapes.

Key Stops:

Flagstaff: A historic city with Route 66 memorabilia and great dining options.

Williams: Known as the "Gateway to the Grand Canyon," featuring old-fashioned diners and shops.

Winslow: Don't miss the "Standin' on the Corner" Park, inspired by the Eagles' famous song.

Seligman: A retro town filled with vintage cars and neon signs.

Highlights:

Meteor Crater: A massive meteorite impact site.

Petrified Forest National Park: Fossilized trees and colorful desert vistas.

Best Time to Drive: Spring and fall for pleasant weather.

Tips:

Allow time for frequent stops; there's a lot to see.

Pack snacks and water, as some stretches are remote.

Other Scenic Drives in Arizona

1. Apache Trail (State Route 88)

Overview: A winding, unpaved road through the rugged Superstition Mountains.

Highlights: Canyon Lake, Tortilla Flat (an old mining town), and stunning desert views.

Length: 40 miles.

Difficulty: Recommended for experienced drivers; not suitable for RVs.

2. Red Rock Scenic Byway (State Route 179)

Overview: A short but awe-inspiring drive in Sedona's Red Rock Country.

Highlights: Bell Rock, Cathedral Rock, and access to numerous hiking trails.

Length: 7.5 miles.

Tips: Stop at designated pullouts for photos.

3. Coronado Trail (US Route 191)

Overview: A remote and winding road through the White Mountains.

Highlights: Alpine forests, volcanic fields, and breathtaking vistas.

Length: 120 miles.

Difficulty: Challenging due to sharp curves and elevation changes.

4. Scenic Loop Drive in Monument Valley

Overview: A dirt road winding through the Navajo Tribal Park's iconic buttes and mesas.

Length: 17 miles.

Fee: $8 per person (as of 2025).

5.5 Camping and Stargazing

Arizona's vast landscapes and clear skies make it a paradise for camping and stargazing enthusiasts. With numerous campgrounds and dark-sky locations, the state offers a perfect escape into nature.

Best Camping Spots

1. Grand Canyon National Park
Options:
Mather Campground (South Rim): $20 per night, reservations required.
North Rim Campground: $25 per night, open seasonally.
Activities: Hiking, ranger talks, and stunning canyon views.
Tips: Bring warm clothing, as temperatures drop at night.
2. Sedona Area
Options:
Manzanita Campground: $22 per night, located near Oak Creek.
Dispersed Camping: Allowed in Coconino National Forest.
Highlights: Red rock formations and serene creekside spots.
3. Lake Powell
Options:
Primitive camping is allowed along the shoreline (free, but permits may be required).
Activities: Boating, fishing, and kayaking.
Tips: Check water levels before planning a trip.
4. Saguaro National Park
Options:
Backcountry camping ($8 per night).
Highlights: Sleep under a canopy of towering saguaro cacti.
5. Kartchner Caverns State Park
Options: $15–$30 per night, with RV hookups and tent sites.
Activities: Cave tours, hiking, and wildlife viewing.

Stargazing in Arizona
Arizona is renowned for its dark skies, making it a prime location for stargazing.
Top Spots:
Flagstaff: The world's first International Dark Sky City, offering observatories and star parties.

Kitt Peak National Observatory (Tucson): Home to nightly stargazing programs.

Meteor Crater RV Park: Far from city lights, offering stunning night skies.

Chiricahua National Monument: Remote and pristine, ideal for amateur astronomers.

Tips for Stargazing

Check moon phases for the darkest nights.

Bring binoculars or a telescope for better views.

Dress warmly; desert nights can be cold.

Use red flashlights to preserve night vision.

Arizona's scenic drives and camping spots let you experience the state's beauty up close, while its dark skies offer unforgettable stargazing moments. Whether exploring Route 66 or camping under a blanket of stars, these adventures are sure to create lifelong memories.

5.6 Hot Air Balloon Rides and Aerial Tours

Soaring above Arizona's stunning landscapes in a hot air balloon or small aircraft is an unforgettable experience. These adventures offer a bird's-eye view of the state's dramatic terrain, from deserts and mountains to canyons and cityscapes.

Hot Air Balloon Rides
Top Locations:
Phoenix and Scottsdale
Overview: Glide over the Sonoran Desert, dotted with saguaros and wildlife.
Companies:
Rainbow Ryders (from $200 per person).
Hot Air Expeditions (from $210 per person).
Experience: Sunrise flights are especially popular, offering cool weather and golden light.

Sedona
Overview: Float above the iconic red rock formations.
Companies:
Red Rock Balloon Adventures (from $250 per person).
Highlights: Views of Cathedral Rock, Bell Rock, and the surrounding canyons.

Tucson
Overview: See the desert landscape framed by the Santa Catalina Mountains.
Companies: Tucson Balloon Rides (from $225 per person).

Tips:
Dress in layers; temperatures can vary.
Book in advance, as flights fill quickly.
Most companies include a celebratory champagne toast after landing.
Aerial Tours
Helicopter and Small Plane Tours
Grand Canyon
Overview: Helicopter rides provide jaw-dropping views of the canyon's depths and width.
Companies:
Maverick Helicopters (from $299 per person).
Papillon Grand Canyon Helicopters (from $279 per person).
Departure Points: South Rim, Las Vegas, or nearby airfields.

Monument Valley
Overview: Scenic flights showcase the towering sandstone buttes.
Cost: From $400 per person for a private tour.
Bonus: Often include a Navajo guide to explain the area's significance.
Lake Powell and Antelope Canyon
Overview: Aerial views reveal the intricate beauty of the lake and slot canyons.
Companies: Grand Canyon Airlines offers tours from $150 per person.
Tips:
Check weight limits and weather conditions before booking.
Morning and late afternoon tours offer the best lighting for photos.

5.7 Rock Climbing and Canyoneering

Arizona's diverse geology provides endless opportunities for rock climbing and canyoneering, from towering cliffs to narrow slot canyons. These activities combine adventure with exploration of the state's hidden gems.

Rock Climbing Spots

Queen Creek Canyon (Near Superior)

Overview: Known for its rugged granite cliffs and routes for all skill levels.

Highlights: "The Pond" area offers shaded climbs.

Gear Rentals: Available in Phoenix ($40–$60 per day).

Mount Lemmon (Tucson)

Overview: Over 1,500 climbing routes spread across different elevations.

Best Season: Spring and fall for mild weather.

Challenges: From beginner-friendly slabs to advanced multi-pitch routes.

Camelback Mountain (Phoenix)

Overview: Popular for bouldering and short climbing routes.

Tips: Start early to avoid heat and crowds.

Canyoneering Adventures

What is Canyoneering?

 Canyoneering involves navigating narrow canyons by hiking, rappelling, swimming, or scrambling over obstacles.

Top Canyoneering Spots

Antelope Canyon (Page)

Overview: Famous for its stunning light beams and smooth sandstone walls.

Tour Requirements: Guided tours only ($70–$100 per person).

Water Holes Canyon (Page)

Overview: A less crowded alternative to Antelope Canyon, featuring beautiful formations and rappelling sections.

Cost: Permit fees start at $12 per person.

Coconino National Forest

Overview: Offers several canyons with varying levels of difficulty, such as West Clear Creek.

Activities: Wading through water and climbing rock faces.

Safety Tips for Climbing and Canyoneering

Always go with a guide if you're new to the area.

Wear proper footwear and gear.

Check the weather forecast; flash floods can occur in canyons.

Pack water, snacks, and a first aid kit.

Whether soaring above the landscapes or delving into canyons, Arizona's adventure activities promise memories for a lifetime. From the thrill of climbing rugged cliffs to the serenity of a hot air balloon ride, there's an adventure for every type of explorer.

Chapter 6: Culture, History, and Local Life

6.1 Native American Heritage and Landmarks

Arizona is a treasure trove of Native American culture and history, offering visitors the chance to connect with ancient traditions, sacred sites, and vibrant communities that have shaped the state for millennia.

Ancestral Legacy

Arizona is home to 22 federally recognized tribes, including the Navajo Nation, Hopi, Apache, and Havasupai peoples. Each tribe has its own rich traditions, languages, and stories that are deeply tied to the land.

Cultural Highlights:

Many tribes offer cultural centers and museums where visitors can learn about their history and heritage.

Traditional crafts such as weaving, pottery, and jewelry-making are often showcased at tribal markets.

Must-Visit Native American Landmarks

1. Monument Valley (Navajo Nation)

Overview: Monument Valley's towering sandstone formations are not only iconic but also deeply sacred to the Navajo people.

What to Do:

Guided Jeep tours with Navajo guides (from $75 per person).

Learn about the legends and traditions tied to the land.

Contact: Monument Valley Navajo Tribal Park Visitor Center.

2. Canyon de Chelly National Monument

Location: Near Chinle, within the Navajo Nation.

Overview: This canyon is home to ancient cliff dwellings and rock art created by the Ancestral Puebloans.

What to Do:

Hike to White House Ruins or take a guided tour (fees from $15 per person).

Listen to stories about the Navajo's connection to this sacred place.

Hours: Sunrise to sunset.

Contact: National Park Service (928-674-5500).

3. Hopi Mesas

Overview: The Hopi villages on the mesas are among the oldest continuously inhabited places in the U.S.

What to Do:

Visit the Hopi Cultural Center to explore exhibits and enjoy Hopi cuisine.

Shop for unique kachina dolls and pottery.

Contact: Hopi Cultural Center (928-734-2401).

4. Havasupai Falls

Overview: Sacred to the Havasupai people, these turquoise waterfalls are a natural wonder.

What to Know:

Permits are required (from $395 per person for a 3-night stay).

Visitors are encouraged to respect the land and traditions of the Havasupai Tribe.

5. Heard Museum (Phoenix)

Overview: A world-class museum dedicated to Native American art and culture.

Exhibits: Traditional art, contemporary works, and exhibits on Native history.

Hours: Daily, 10 AM–4 PM.

Admission: $20 for adults, $9 for children.

Contact: (602-252-8840).

Cultural Experiences

Powwows and Festivals

Many tribes host powwows, featuring dance, music, and storytelling.

Notable Event: The Heard Museum Guild Indian Fair & Market (March).

Guided Tours by Tribes

Engage directly with Native guides for authentic experiences.

Example: Navajo-guided tours of Antelope Canyon.

Artisan Markets

Locations like Old Town Scottsdale feature Native American art, from turquoise jewelry to handwoven rugs.

Tips for Visitors

Respect Sacred Sites: Some areas may have restricted access or require permits. Always follow guidelines provided by tribal authorities.

Support Local Communities: Purchasing directly from Native artists and businesses helps sustain their economies.

Learn and Listen: Take the opportunity to hear stories and teachings shared by tribal members to deepen your understanding.

Exploring Arizona's Native American heritage offers more than a journey through history—it's a chance to connect with living cultures and landscapes that hold profound meaning. These experiences will enrich your visit and leave you with a deep appreciation for the traditions that shape the Grand Canyon State.

6.2 Old West Towns and Historic Sites

Arizona's rugged desert landscapes once served as the backdrop for the Old West, a time of cowboys, gunfights, and gold rushes. Today, visitors can step back in time and experience this fascinating era through preserved towns, historical landmarks, and reenactments.

Top Old West Towns
1. Tombstone
Overview: Known as "The Town Too Tough to Die," Tombstone was a hub of lawlessness and gold fever in the late 1800s.

Must-See Attractions:
OK Corral: Witness a reenactment of the famous 1881 gunfight ($10 admission).
Bird Cage Theatre: Explore this historic saloon and brothel, now a museum.
Boothill Graveyard: Visit the final resting place of outlaws and gunslingers.
Hours: Most attractions open daily, 9 AM–5 PM.
Contact: Tombstone Chamber of Commerce (520-457-9317).

2. Bisbee
Overview: A former mining town nestled in the Mule Mountains, Bisbee is now a charming arts community.
What to Do:
Take a tour of the Queen Mine ($14 per person).
Stroll through historic Brewery Gulch for unique shops and cafes.
Hours: Queen Mine Tours run daily, 9 AM–4 PM.
Contact: Bisbee Visitor Center (520-432-3554).

3. Prescott
Overview: Once Arizona's territorial capital, Prescott retains its Old West charm.
Highlights:
Whiskey Row: A historic street lined with saloons, galleries, and restaurants.
Sharlot Hall Museum: Discover Arizona's early history through exhibits and preserved buildings.
Contact: Prescott Chamber of Commerce (928-445-2000).

Historic Sites and Landmarks
1. Jerome
Overview: A ghost town turned artist haven, Jerome was once a booming copper mining town.
What to Do:
Visit the Jerome State Historic Park to learn about the town's mining history.

Explore the eerie remains of abandoned buildings.
Contact: Jerome Chamber of Commerce (928-634-2900).
2. Yuma Territorial Prison
Overview: Once a prison for Arizona's most notorious criminals, now a state historic park.

Admission: $8 for adults, $4 for children.
Contact: Yuma Territorial Prison Museum (928-783-4771).

3. Fort Apache Historic Park
Overview: This site highlights both military and Native American history.
What to See:
The original fort buildings.
The nearby White Mountain Apache Cultural Center and Museum.
Contact: Fort Apache Visitor Center (928-338-1230).
Tips for Visiting Old West Towns

Plan for Crowds: Popular towns like Tombstone can get busy on weekends and during festivals.
Wear Comfortable Shoes: Many historic towns feature dirt roads and uneven paths.
Support Local Businesses: From handmade goods to guided tours, spending locally helps preserve these landmarks.

6.3 Arts and Music Scene

Arizona's arts and music scene is as diverse as its landscapes, blending Native American traditions, Old West influences, and contemporary creativity. Whether you're exploring vibrant galleries or attending a music festival under the desert stars, the state offers something for every art lover.
Arts in Arizona

1. Scottsdale's Art District
Overview: A hub for fine art galleries, showcasing everything from Native American crafts to modern masterpieces.
Don't Miss:
Scottsdale ArtWalk (Thursday evenings).
The Western Spirit: Scottsdale's Museum of the West.
Contact: Scottsdale Gallery Association (480-990-3939).
2. Sedona's Art Scene

Overview: Sedona's dramatic red rocks have inspired artists for generations.
Highlights:

Tlaquepaque Arts & Crafts Village: A charming shopping area with galleries and workshops.

Sedona International Film Festival (February).
Contact: Sedona Arts Center (928-282-3809).
3. Tucson's Mural Movement
Overview: Tucson has embraced street art, with colorful murals adorning its historic downtown.
What to Do: Take a self-guided walking tour of the murals or join a local tour group.
Music in Arizona
1. Flagstaff Music Scene
Overview: Flagstaff offers a mix of live music venues, from cozy coffee shops to lively bars.
Events:
Flagstaff Folk Festival (June).
Orpheum Theater hosts indie and folk bands.
2. Arizona Jazz Festival
Location: Phoenix.
Overview: A renowned event featuring top jazz performers from around the world.
Dates: Held annually in April.
3. Native American Music
Experience traditional drumming and chanting at cultural festivals and powwows across the state.
Tips for Enjoying Arizona's Arts and Music
Check Event Schedules: Many festivals and concerts require advance tickets.
Visit Local Galleries: Small towns often have hidden gems showcasing regional art.
Engage with Artists: Many galleries and events allow you to meet the creators and learn about their work.
Arizona's vibrant arts and music scene offers an enriching contrast to its rugged outdoor adventures, ensuring a well-rounded travel experience.

6.4 Local Traditions and Festivals

Arizona is a melting pot of cultures and traditions, with influences from Native American tribes, Hispanic communities, and Old West heritage. These rich traditions are celebrated through festivals, events, and daily life, offering visitors a chance to experience the state's unique spirit.

Traditional Events

1. Powwows and Tribal Celebrations

Overview: Arizona is home to 22 Native American tribes, each with unique cultural traditions. Powwows feature drumming, dancing, and storytelling, showcasing indigenous heritage.

Key Event: Heard Museum Guild Indian Fair & Market (Phoenix)

What to Expect: Art, food, and performances from various tribes.

When: March.

Contact: Heard Museum (602-252-8848).

2. Hispanic Celebrations

Día de los Muertos (Day of the Dead)

Overview: A vibrant cultural festival honoring deceased loved ones.

Where: Tucson and Phoenix host large-scale celebrations.

Highlights: Altars, marigolds, traditional food, and live music.

Seasonal Festivals

1. Arizona State Fair

Location: Phoenix.

Overview: A month-long fair with rides, food, concerts, and exhibits.

When: October.

Admission: $15 for adults, $10 for children.

2. Tucson Rodeo (La Fiesta de los Vaqueros)

Overview: This Old West tradition celebrates Arizona's cowboy heritage.

What to See: Bull riding, barrel racing, and parades.

When: February.

Contact: Tucson Rodeo Office (520-741-2233).

Cultural Experiences

Cultural Dance Performances: Many resorts and cultural centers feature traditional dances, such as the Hopi Butterfly Dance or Navajo Yei Bi Chei dance.

Local Food Traditions: Sample fry bread, tamales, and mesquite-flavored dishes at cultural fairs.

Tips for Enjoying Festivals

Plan Ahead: Popular events can sell out, so buy tickets early.

Dress for the Weather: Many events are outdoors, so bring sunscreen and hats.

Engage with Locals: Festivals are a great time to meet Arizonans and learn about their traditions.

6.5 Arizona's Mining History and Ghost Towns

Arizona's history is deeply rooted in mining, with gold, silver, and copper fueling its early economy. Today, remnants of this era can be explored through ghost towns, historic mines, and museums scattered across the state.

Key Mining Towns and Ghost Towns

1. Jerome

Overview: Once called the "Wickedest Town in the West," Jerome was a bustling copper mining town. Now, it's an artsy ghost town with a spooky charm.

What to See:

Jerome State Historic Park: Learn about mining life through exhibits.

Sliding Jail: A jail that moved downhill due to shifting earth!

Contact: Jerome Chamber of Commerce (928-634-2900).

2. Bisbee

Overview: Known for its rich copper deposits, Bisbee has evolved into a quirky artist enclave.

What to Do:

Queen Mine Tour: Go underground and explore an actual mine ($14 per person).

Stroll through Brewery Gulch for unique shops and restaurants.

Contact: Bisbee Visitor Center (520-432-3554).

3. Goldfield Ghost Town

Location: Near Apache Junction.

Overview: A restored ghost town with a mix of authentic and reconstructed buildings.

What to Do:

Take a mine tour or ride the narrow-gauge railroad.

Watch an Old West gunfight reenactment.

Admission: Free entry; activities cost $3–$10.

Mining History Museums

1. Arizona Mining and Mineral Museum (Phoenix)

Overview: Discover Arizona's mineral wealth and mining tools.

Admission: Free.
Contact: Arizona Historical Society (602-771-1600).
2. Bisbee Mining & Historical Museum
Overview: A Smithsonian-affiliated museum exploring Bisbee's mining heyday.
Admission: $10 for adults, $4 for children.
Contact: 520-432-7071.

Tips for Exploring Ghost Towns
Respect the Sites: Many ghost towns are fragile and should be treated with care.
Wear Sturdy Shoes: Uneven terrain and old buildings can be tricky to navigate.
Bring Cash: Smaller towns may not accept credit cards.
Arizona's mining history and ghost towns provide a fascinating glimpse into the state's rugged past, offering an unforgettable journey through time.

6.6 Cultural Centers and Museums

Arizona boasts a rich tapestry of cultural experiences, celebrated in its numerous cultural centers and museums. These institutions highlight Native American heritage, Hispanic influences, the Old West, and the state's natural history. Whether you're a history buff, art lover, or simply curious, Arizona's museums offer something for everyone.

Key Cultural Centers
1. Heard Museum
Location: Phoenix.
Overview: Dedicated to Native American cultures, this world-renowned museum features art, jewelry, textiles, and immersive exhibits.
Highlights:
"**HOME:** Native Peoples of the Southwest" Exhibit: Explore the stories, traditions, and history of Arizona's tribes.
Annual Indian Fair & Market: A vibrant celebration of Native American art and culture.
Admission: $20 adults, $9 children (6–17), free for under 6.
Contact: (602-252-8848) | Heard Museum Website.
Hours: Open daily, 9:30 AM – 5:00 PM.

2. Pueblo Grande Museum and Archaeological Park

Location: Phoenix.

Overview: Explore the ruins of a 1,500-year-old Hohokam village.

What to Do:

Stroll the interpretive trail around ancient canals and platform mounds.

Visit the museum for artifacts and cultural insights.

Admission: $6 adults, $3 children (6–17), free for under 6.

Contact: (602-495-0901).

Hours: Monday–Saturday, 9:00 AM – 4:45 PM; Sunday, 1:00 PM – 4:45 PM.

3. Mission San Xavier del Bac

Location: Tucson.

Overview: A stunning Spanish mission built in the late 1700s, often called the "White Dove of the Desert."

Highlights:

Guided tours detailing its history and architecture.

Serene atmosphere ideal for reflection.

Admission: Free (donations accepted).

Contact: (520-294-2624).

Hours: Open daily, 9:00 AM – 4:00 PM.

Major Museums to Visit

1. Arizona-Sonora Desert Museum

Location: Tucson.

Overview: Part zoo, part botanical garden, part natural history museum, this unique facility celebrates the Sonoran Desert.

Highlights:

Live animal exhibits featuring mountain lions, javelinas, and more.

Desert trails with over 1,200 native plant species.

Admission: $25.95 adults, $13.95 children (3–12).

Contact: (520-883-2702).

Hours: Open daily, 7:30 AM – 5:00 PM.

2. Musical Instrument Museum (MIM)

Location: Phoenix.

Overview: A global journey through music, featuring over 8,000 instruments from around the world.

Highlights:
Interactive exhibits where visitors can play instruments.

Performances in the on-site concert hall.
Admission: $20 adults, $15 teens (13–19), $10 children (4–12).
Contact: (480-478-6000).
Hours: Open daily, 9:00 AM – 5:00 PM.
3. Lowell Observatory
Location: Flagstaff.
Overview: This historic observatory is where Pluto was discovered in 1930.
What to Do:
Attend stargazing events and guided telescope tours.
Learn about the universe in the interactive exhibits.
Admission: $25 adults, $16 children (5–17), free for under 5.
Contact: (928-774-3358).
Hours: Open daily, 10:00 AM – 10:00 PM.
Unique Experiences
Western Spirit: Scottsdale's Museum of the West

Celebrate Arizona's cowboy culture through art, artifacts, and interactive exhibits.
Admission: $20 adults, $9 children (6–17).
Titan Missile Museum (Green Valley)
Tour an actual Cold War missile site and learn about nuclear deterrence.
Admission: $15 adults, $10 children (6–12).
Meteor Crater (Winslow)
Visit one of the best-preserved meteor impact sites in the world.
Admission: $25 adults, $16 children (6–17).
Tips for Visiting Cultural Centers and Museums
Plan Ahead: Check websites or call to confirm hours and ticket prices.
Bring Comfortable Shoes: Many museums include outdoor exhibits or walking trails.
Look for Discounts: Some museums offer free admission days or reduced prices for students, seniors, or military personnel.
Engage with Staff: Docents and tour guides can provide deeper insights and personal stories.

Arizona's cultural centers and museums offer a window into its rich and diverse history, making them must-visit destinations for any traveler.

Chapter 7: Where to Stay

7.1 Hotels and Resorts

Arizona offers a variety of accommodations, from luxury resorts to budget-friendly hotels. Each option provides a unique experience, catering to different preferences and budgets. Whether you're seeking a spa retreat, a family-friendly stay, or proximity to iconic attractions, you'll find the perfect lodging in the Grand Canyon State.

Luxury Resorts

1. The Phoenician

Location: Scottsdale.

Overview: A luxurious resort known for its world-class amenities, including golf courses, a spa, and fine dining.

Highlights:

Multiple pools with private cabanas.

Stunning views of Camelback Mountain.

Price Range: From $600 per night.

Contact: (480-941-8200).

Address: 6000 E Camelback Rd, Scottsdale, AZ 85251.

2. Enchantment Resort

Location: Sedona.

Overview: Nestled among the red rocks, this resort offers a tranquil escape with an emphasis on wellness.

Highlights:

On-site Mii amo Spa.

Guided hikes and yoga sessions.

Price Range: From $700 per night.

Contact: (928-282-2900).

Address: 525 Boynton Canyon Rd, Sedona, AZ 86336.

Mid-Range Hotels

1. SpringHill Suites by Marriott

Location: Flagstaff.

Overview: A comfortable option near the downtown area and close to attractions like Lowell Observatory.
Highlights:

Complimentary breakfast.
Indoor pool and fitness center.
Price Range: From $180 per night.
Contact: (928-774-8042).
Address: 2455 S Beulah Blvd, Flagstaff, AZ 86001.

2. Hotel Congress
Location: Tucson.
Overview: A historic boutique hotel with vintage charm and a lively atmosphere.
Highlights:
On-site nightclub and restaurant.
A hotspot for live music events.
Price Range: From $150 per night.
Contact: (520-622-8848).
Address: 311 E Congress St, Tucson, AZ 85701.

Budget-Friendly Options
1. Super 8 by Wyndham
Location: Page/Lake Powell.
Overview: A wallet-friendly option close to Antelope Canyon and Horseshoe Bend.
Highlights:
Free breakfast and parking.
Comfortable rooms with basic amenities.
Price Range: From $90 per night.
Contact: (928-645-5858).
Address: 649 S Lake Powell Blvd, Page, AZ 86040.

2. Red Roof Inn
Location: Phoenix.
Overview: An affordable stay for budget-conscious travelers exploring the city.
Highlights:
Pet-friendly accommodations.
Free Wi-Fi and parking.
Price Range: From $80 per night.

Contact: (602-275-7601).

Address: 2135 W 15th St, Tempe, AZ 85281.

Family-Friendly Stays

1. Great Wolf Lodge

Location: Scottsdale.

Overview: A family-focused resort with an indoor water park and plenty of kid-friendly activities.

Highlights:

Interactive games and activities for children.

Multiple dining options on-site.

Price Range: From $250 per night.

Contact: (844-473-9653).

Address: 7333 N Pima Rd, Scottsdale, AZ 85258.

2. Embassy Suites by Hilton

Location: Phoenix.

Overview: Known for spacious suites, ideal for families.

Highlights:

Complimentary evening reception.

Free cooked-to-order breakfast.

Price Range: From $170 per night.

Contact: (602-765-5800).

Address: 4415 E Paradise Village Pkwy S, Phoenix, AZ 85032.

Tips for Choosing Accommodations

Book Early: Especially for high-demand areas like Sedona and the Grand Canyon.

Look for Deals: Off-season travel can result in significant savings.

Check Reviews: Online reviews can provide insight into cleanliness, service, and amenities.

Consider Location: Staying near attractions can save time and travel costs.

Arizona's diverse accommodations ensure a comfortable and memorable stay, no matter your budget or preferences. From luxury resorts to cozy inns, there's something for everyone in the Grand Canyon State!

7.2 Bed and Breakfasts

For travelers seeking a cozy and personalized experience, Arizona's bed and breakfasts (B&Bs) are the perfect choice. These intimate lodgings often feature charming décor, homemade breakfasts, and local hospitality.

Top Bed and Breakfasts in Arizona
1. Canyon Villa Bed and Breakfast
Location: Sedona.
Overview: Overlooking the iconic red rocks, this B&B offers stunning views and a peaceful retreat.
Highlights:
Gourmet breakfast served daily.
Outdoor pool and garden.
Price Range: From $300 per night.
Contact: (928-282-3365).
Address: 40 Canyon Circle Dr, Sedona, AZ 86351.
2. England House Bed and Breakfast

Location: Flagstaff.
Overview: A historic Victorian home transformed into a delightful B&B, perfect for exploring the Grand Canyon or downtown Flagstaff.
Highlights:
Unique themed rooms.
Complimentary evening snacks.
Price Range: From $200 per night.
Contact: (928-214-7350).
Address: 614 W Santa Fe Ave, Flagstaff, AZ 86001.

3. Inn at 410 Bed and Breakfast
Location: Flagstaff.
Overview: Known for its cozy atmosphere and elegant rooms, this B&B is a favorite among couples.
Highlights:
Full breakfast with vegetarian options.
On-site concierge service for local activities.
Price Range: From $180 per night.

Contact: (928-774-0088).

Address: 410 N Leroux St, Flagstaff, AZ 86001.

7.3 Vacation Rentals and Cabins

Vacation rentals and cabins offer flexibility and privacy, ideal for families, groups, or those who prefer a home-like setting. Arizona provides a range of options, from rustic cabins in the mountains to luxurious desert homes with pools.

Popular Vacation Rentals

1. Sedona Red Rock Retreat

Location: Sedona.

Overview: A modern home with panoramic views of the red rocks.

Highlights:

Full kitchen and outdoor BBQ area.

Close to hiking trails and local shops.

Price Range: From $250 per night.

2. Grand Canyon Cabin

Location: Williams.

Overview: A cozy cabin surrounded by pine forests, perfect for Grand Canyon visitors.

Highlights:

Fireplace and outdoor deck.

Pet-friendly option available.

Price Range: From $150 per night.

3. Scottsdale Desert Villa

Location: Scottsdale.

Overview: A spacious villa with modern amenities, including a private pool and outdoor lounge area.

Highlights:

Great for groups and families.

Close to golf courses and shopping.

Price Range: From $400 per night.

Rustic Cabins

1. Pinewood Cabins

Location: Payson.

Overview: Quaint cabins nestled in the Mogollon Rim, ideal for nature lovers.
Highlights:
Fully equipped kitchen.
Access to hiking trails and fishing spots.
Price Range: From $120 per night.

2. Greer Lodge Resort & Cabins
Location: Greer.
Overview: A serene mountain retreat offering picturesque views and peaceful surroundings.
Highlights:
Options range from one-bedroom cabins to large family lodges.
Great for fishing and wildlife watching.
Price Range: From $160 per night.
Contact: (928-735-7216).
Address: 80 Main St, Greer, AZ 85927.

Tips for Booking
Book Early: Rentals near popular attractions, like the Grand Canyon, fill up quickly.
Read Reviews: Check guest feedback to ensure quality and comfort.
Ask About Amenities: Confirm features like Wi-Fi, parking, and pet policies before booking.
Look for Deals: Off-season stays often come with discounts.
Whether you're looking for a charming B&B or a private vacation rental, Arizona has the perfect lodging option to make your stay unforgettable.

7.4 Camping Grounds

Camping in Arizona offers a chance to connect with the state's natural beauty, from desert landscapes to towering pines and red rock formations. Whether you prefer traditional camping or glamping (luxury camping), Arizona provides various campgrounds catering to different needs and levels of adventure.

Top Camping Grounds in Arizona
1. Grand Canyon National Park Campground
Location: Grand Canyon.

Overview: Offering stunning views of the Grand Canyon, this campground provides both tent and RV sites.

Highlights:

Proximity to hiking trails and breathtaking vistas.

Campsites with picnic tables and fire rings.

Price Range: From $18 per night (tent sites).

Contact: (928-638-7888).

Address: Grand Canyon Village, Grand Canyon, AZ 86023.

2. Lost Dutchman State Park

Location: Apache Junction.

Overview: A desert campground with incredible views of the Superstition Mountains.

Highlights:

Scenic hiking and wildlife watching.

Accessible RV sites with full hookups.

Price Range: From $30 per night (tent sites).

Contact: (602-601-1993).

Address: 6109 N Apache Trail, Apache Junction, AZ 85119.

3. Petrified Forest National Park Campground

Location: Holbrook.

Overview: A unique camping experience with ancient fossils and a range of hiking opportunities.

Highlights:

Close proximity to the park's famous petrified wood.

Quiet, star-filled nights for stargazing.

Price Range: From $20 per night (tent sites).

Contact: (928-524-6228).

Address: 1 Park Rd, Petrified Forest, AZ 86028.

4. Mather Campground

Location: Grand Canyon.

Overview: A more developed campground with amenities like showers and food storage.

Highlights:

Shaded sites for tent camping.

Located near the South Rim, offering easy access to popular Grand Canyon viewpoints.
Price Range: From $18 per night (tent sites).
Contact: (928-638-7888).
Address: Grand Canyon Village, Grand Canyon, AZ 86023.

7.5 Unique Stays: Yurts, Ranches, and Glamping

If you're looking for something a bit different than the traditional hotel or campsite, Arizona's unique stays offer a blend of adventure and comfort. From glamping in luxurious tents to staying in a rustic ranch or a cozy yurt, these options make your stay in Arizona even more memorable.

Unique Stay Options
1. Under Canvas Grand Canyon (Glamping)
Location: Near Grand Canyon National Park.
Overview: Experience the beauty of the desert in a glamorous tent equipped with comfortable beds and electricity.

Highlights:
Luxury tents with private bathrooms and outdoor showers.
Stargazing opportunities and campfire circles.
Price Range: From $250 per night.
Contact: (877-786-4386).
Address: 19 Miles South of Grand Canyon Village, Grand Canyon, AZ 86023.

2. The Ranch at Fossil Creek
Location: Strawberry.
Overview: A working ranch offering cabins, yurts, and horseback riding experiences.
Highlights:
Horseback riding and fishing.
Ranch-to-table dining with locally sourced ingredients.
Price Range: From $175 per night for yurts.
Contact: (928-476-4232).
Address: 2064 E Fossil Creek Rd, Strawberry, AZ 85544.
3. Glamping at Sedona Village

Location: Sedona.

Overview: Enjoy a luxurious outdoor experience in Sedona's stunning Red Rock Country, staying in comfortable, fully furnished tents.

Highlights:

Tents with queen-size beds and electricity.

Complimentary breakfast and hiking excursions.

Price Range: From $225 per night.

Contact: (928-282-5200).

Address: 3100 State Route 89A, Sedona, AZ 86336.

4. Yurt at Verde Valley

Location: Camp Verde.

Overview: Stay in a yurt surrounded by beautiful desert landscapes, offering a unique blend of comfort and outdoor living.

Highlights:

Yurts with wooden floors, full kitchens, and air conditioning.

Enjoy access to hiking, fishing, and wildlife watching.

Price Range: From $125 per night.

Contact: (928-567-8777).

Address: 2800 W. Finnie Flat Rd, Camp Verde, AZ 86322.

Tips for Unique Stays

Book in Advance: Unique stays like glamping and yurts can be popular, especially during peak seasons, so it's best to secure your spot early.

Pack Light: While these unique stays offer comfort, it's always best to pack light and bring your essentials.

Check for Seasonal Availability: Some glamping sites and ranches are seasonal, so make sure they are open when you plan to visit.

Whether you're looking for a luxurious glamping experience, a ranch stay for the full Arizona adventure, or a peaceful yurt in the wilderness, Arizona offers a wide range of unique accommodations that will make your visit unforgettable.

Chapter 8: Dining and Local Flavors

8.1 Classic Southwestern Cuisine

Arizona's food scene is deeply influenced by its Southwestern roots, blending flavors from Native American, Mexican, and Spanish cuisines. Whether you're enjoying a meal in Phoenix or a cozy restaurant in the desert, you'll find a wide array of bold, flavorful dishes that are unique to the region. Classic Southwestern cuisine is defined by the use of fresh ingredients, fiery spices, and a focus on comfort foods that reflect the state's cultural melting pot.

Signature Dishes of Southwestern Arizona

1. Chimichangas

Description: A deep-fried burrito that's crispy on the outside and packed with flavor on the inside. Often filled with beef, chicken, or beans and rice, chimichangas are a must-try in Arizona.

Where to Try: Many Southwestern restaurants, including local favorite Chuy's Mesquite Broiler in Tucson.

2. Sonoran Hot Dogs

Description: A regional twist on the classic hot dog, this version is wrapped in bacon and topped with pinto beans, tomatoes, onions, jalapeños, and a special sauce, all inside a soft, fluffy bun. It's a true Arizona street food.

Where to Try: El Guero Canelo in Tucson is known for its amazing Sonoran hot dogs.

3. Carne Adovada

Description: A flavorful slow-cooked pork dish marinated in a rich blend of red chilies and spices. It's commonly served with rice, beans, and tortillas.

Where to Try: Los Dos Molinos in Phoenix offers an excellent version of carne adovada.

4. Navajo Tacos

Description: A delicious dish made with fry bread topped with seasoned ground beef or chicken, lettuce, cheese, salsa, and sour cream. It's a traditional Native American dish that has become a beloved favorite across the state.

Where to Try: Tuba City Trading Post on the Navajo Nation offers some of the best Navajo tacos in the region.

5. Mesquite-Grilled Meats

Description: Mesquite wood is often used to grill meats in Arizona, imparting a smoky flavor to dishes like steaks, chicken, and even fish. Grilled meats are a staple of Arizona's Southwestern dining.

Where to Try: The Ranch House Grille in Phoenix serves mesquite-grilled steaks and other delicious cuts of meat.

6. Green Chile Stew

Description: This hearty stew is made with green chile peppers, pork, potatoes, and other vegetables, offering a smoky and spicy flavor that reflects the Southwestern palette.

Where to Try: Los Dos Molinos in Phoenix serves an incredible green chile stew.

Popular Ingredients in Southwestern Cuisine

Chilies: Arizona's cuisine heavily features chilies, from mild to fiery, adding heat and depth to many dishes. The state is known for its green chiles, red chiles, and even chipotle peppers.

Corn: Corn is a staple, often used in tortillas, tamales, and various sides. It's one of the earliest crops cultivated by Native Americans and remains a key part of the diet today.

Beans: Pinto beans and black beans are commonly featured in Southwestern meals, from burritos to stews.

Cheese: Mexican cheese varieties, such as queso fresco and cotija, are often sprinkled on top of dishes for added flavor.

Squash: The desert's warm climate makes it ideal for growing squash, which is often used in stews and as a side dish.

Where to Experience Classic Southwestern Dining

1. Pizzeria Bianco (Phoenix)

Why Go: While Arizona isn't necessarily known for pizza, Pizzeria Bianco offers an unforgettable experience with its wood-fired pizzas that blend Southwestern ingredients.

Address: 623 E Adams St, Phoenix, AZ 85004.

2. Taco Guild (Phoenix)

Why Go: Located in a historic church, Taco Guild elevates the humble taco with creative fillings and locally sourced ingredients. It's a popular spot to taste some of Arizona's finest tacos.

Address: 1516 E. McKinley St, Phoenix, AZ 85006.

3. The Mission (Scottsdale)

Why Go: For a fine-dining take on traditional Southwestern cuisine, The Mission offers a sophisticated atmosphere and upscale versions of dishes like tacos, carne asada, and their famous tableside guacamole.

Address: 3815 N. Brown Ave, Scottsdale, AZ 85251.

4. Geronimo (Sedona)

Why Go: A restaurant that combines fine dining with Southwestern influences, Geronimo offers a unique blend of flavors, with dishes like pecan-crusted rack of lamb and roasted chile-rubbed filet mignon.

Address: 2515 W State Rte 89A, Sedona, AZ 86336.

5. Bobby Q (Phoenix)

Why Go: A casual spot for enjoying slow-cooked, smoky barbecue, Bobby Q is famous for its mesquite-grilled meats and hearty sides.

Address: 8501 N 27th Ave, Phoenix, AZ 85051.

A Dining Experience to Remember

When dining in Arizona, make sure to try the authentic Southwestern dishes that define the state's culinary landscape. The bold flavors, creative fusions, and local ingredients will give you a true taste of the Grand Canyon State. Whether you're enjoying street food or fine dining, the food in Arizona is as much of an adventure as the landscapes that surround it!

8.2 Farm-to-Table Restaurants

Arizona's farm-to-table movement has gained a lot of traction over the years, with chefs and restaurants focusing on locally sourced ingredients to create fresh and flavorful dishes. With its diverse agricultural landscape, the state offers a variety of produce, meats, and dairy products that make its farm-to-table dining experiences unique. From urban restaurants to countryside eateries, the farm-to-table ethos is central to many dining establishments.

Top Farm-to-Table Restaurants in Arizona
1. The Farm at South Mountain (Phoenix)
Description: Located in the heart of Phoenix, The Farm at South Mountain offers a peaceful oasis where guests can dine in a beautiful garden setting. The restaurant

features a menu inspired by the seasons, using fresh produce grown on the property and sourced from local farms.

Menu Highlights: Seasonal salads, roasted vegetables, and herb-infused dishes.

Address: 6106 S 32nd St, Phoenix, AZ 85042.

2. The Joy Bus Diner (Phoenix)

Description: This charming diner focuses on fresh, local ingredients, with the added benefit of supporting a great cause. All the proceeds from The Joy Bus Diner go toward supporting homebound cancer patients. The menu changes seasonally based on the availability of local ingredients.

Menu Highlights: Breakfast burritos, seasonal fruit bowls, and fresh salads.

Address: 3375 E Shea Blvd, Phoenix, AZ 85028.

3. Beckett's Table (Scottsdale)

Description: Beckett's Table is known for its upscale comfort food with a strong focus on Arizona-grown produce. The restaurant has built relationships with local farms to ensure the freshest ingredients are used in their dishes.

Menu Highlights: Braised short ribs, seasonal vegetables, and roasted chicken.

Address: 3717 E Indian School Rd, Phoenix, AZ 85018.

4. Cotton & Copper (Phoenix)

Description: A relatively new addition to the Arizona food scene, Cotton & Copper offers contemporary American dishes with a farm-to-table approach. They focus on sustainability and sourcing from local farms to create dishes that highlight the flavors of the region.

Menu Highlights: Grilled meats, seasonal salads, and fresh fish.

Address: 1500 E Van Buren St, Phoenix, AZ 85006.

5. Cafe Zupas (Mesa)

Description: Although Cafe Zupas is a more casual spot, they emphasize fresh, local ingredients in their soups, salads, and sandwiches. The restaurant prides itself on being able to create vibrant dishes using ingredients from Arizona farms.

Menu Highlights: Fresh soups, gourmet salads, and grilled sandwiches.

Address: 4445 E Ray Rd, Phoenix, AZ 85044.

Benefits of Farm-to-Table Dining

Freshness: Farm-to-table restaurants focus on offering ingredients that are in season, which means your meals will taste fresher and be packed with nutrients.

Supporting Local Farmers: When you eat at a farm-to-table restaurant, you're supporting local farmers and helping to maintain the state's agricultural traditions.

Sustainability: Many farm-to-table restaurants in Arizona prioritize sustainability by sourcing organic ingredients, reducing food waste, and minimizing their carbon footprint.

Healthier Options: Locally sourced ingredients tend to be fresher and less processed, which means you're eating healthier meals with fewer additives and preservatives.

8.3 Must-Try Dishes and Regional Favorites

No visit to Arizona would be complete without sampling some of the state's signature dishes. Arizona cuisine is a blend of Native American, Mexican, and Western influences, and its rich history is reflected in every bite. Whether you're trying street food or dining in a fine restaurant, there are several dishes and regional favorites you simply can't miss.

Must-Try Dishes in Arizona

1. Sonoran Hot Dog

Description: This is the ultimate Arizona street food. The Sonoran hot dog is a beef hot dog wrapped in bacon, then topped with pinto beans, tomatoes, onions, jalapeños, mustard, and mayonnaise. It's served in a soft, lightly toasted roll, creating a delicious blend of flavors and textures.

Where to Try: El Guero Canelo (Tucson) and The Sonoran Dog (Phoenix).

2. Carne Asada Fries

Description: A Tex-Mex dish that has become a fan favorite, carne asada fries feature crispy French fries topped with tender marinated beef, cheese, guacamole, sour cream, and salsa. It's a savory, satisfying meal that's perfect for sharing.

Where to Try: Los Dos Molinos (Phoenix) and Carne Asada Express (Tucson).

3. Navajo Taco

Description: A Navajo taco is a fried dough base (similar to a thick, soft tortilla) topped with seasoned ground beef or chicken, lettuce, cheese, salsa, and sour cream. It's a hearty, delicious meal that's a perfect representation of Native American cuisine.

Where to Try: Tuba City Trading Post (Navajo Nation) and Navajo Cultural Center (Window Rock).

4. Green Chile Stew

Description: This hearty stew features green chiles, pork, and potatoes, simmered to create a smoky, spicy, and comforting dish. It's a popular dish during the cooler months and is often served with rice or tortillas.

Where to Try: Los Dos Molinos (Phoenix) and El Pinto (Tucson).

5. Chiles Rellenos

Description: A classic Mexican dish, chiles rellenos are large, mild green chiles stuffed with cheese, meat, or beans, then battered and fried. The dish is often served with a rich tomato sauce and is a must-try in Arizona.

Where to Try: The Mission (Scottsdale) and Taco Guild (Phoenix).

6. Mesquite-Grilled Meats

Description: Mesquite wood is widely used in Arizona for grilling meats, infusing them with a distinct smoky flavor. Whether you're eating steaks, chicken, or pork, mesquite grilling creates tender, flavorful meat dishes.

Where to Try: The Ranch House Grille (Phoenix) and Bobby Q (Phoenix).

7. Prickly Pear Cactus

Description: Prickly pear cactus is a unique and iconic ingredient in Arizona cuisine. It can be eaten raw or cooked, and it's often used in salsas, jellies, and cocktails.

Where to Try: The Desert Bistro (Sedona) and Bobby Q (Phoenix).

Regional Favorites and Sweets

1. Fry Bread

Description: A beloved Native American food, fry bread is a deep-fried dough that's soft and slightly crispy on the edges. It's often served with honey or used as a base for Navajo tacos.

Where to Try: Tuba City Trading Post (Navajo Nation) and The Frybread House (Phoenix).

2. Mesquite Bean Ice Cream

Description: Mesquite beans are ground into a powder and used in a variety of desserts, including ice cream. This unique flavor is a true taste of the desert and is a fun way to try a local delicacy.

Where to Try: Sweet Republic (Scottsdale) and The Gelato Spot (Tempe).

A Culinary Adventure in Arizona

The dishes of Arizona reflect the diversity of its culture and history, and eating your way through the state is a true adventure. From street food to high-end restaurants, the bold flavors and creative takes on traditional Southwestern ingredients will leave you craving more. Whether you're tasting the smoky mesquite meats or trying a unique desert fruit like prickly pear, you'll experience a truly unforgettable culinary journey in Arizona.

8.4 Food Festivals and Farmers' Markets

Arizona's food scene is not only diverse in flavors but also vibrant in its celebrations. The state hosts numerous food festivals and farmers' markets throughout the year, offering visitors the chance to indulge in fresh, locally sourced produce, specialty foods, and unique culinary creations. These events are the perfect way to experience Arizona's rich agricultural heritage, seasonal offerings, and lively community spirit.

Top Food Festivals in Arizona

1. The Arizona Farm & Food Festival (Phoenix)

Description: This annual festival is a celebration of Arizona's agricultural bounty, featuring over 100 local vendors, farmers, and food artisans. It's an opportunity to sample some of the state's best homegrown produce, meats, and cheeses, as well as artisanal breads, pastries, and handmade treats.

What to Expect: Cooking demonstrations, food tastings, and live music.

When: Typically held in March or April.

Location: Various locations in Phoenix.

Cost: $10–$20 per person (depends on entry type).

2. Tucson Meet Yourself (Tucson)

Description: Tucson Meet Yourself is a vibrant cultural festival that showcases Tucson's diverse food and arts scene. The event features over 40 food vendors, many of whom offer traditional Mexican, Native American, and Southwestern dishes.

What to Expect: A variety of food trucks, live entertainment, cultural performances, and handmade arts and crafts.

When: Held in October.

Location: Downtown Tucson.

Cost: Free entry; food and activities available for purchase.

3. The Scottsdale Culinary Festival (Scottsdale)

Description: One of Arizona's oldest food festivals, the Scottsdale Culinary Festival is a premier event that brings together top chefs, local restaurants, and food enthusiasts. It's a chance to sample signature dishes from Arizona's finest dining establishments while enjoying music, art, and family-friendly activities.

What to Expect: food pairings, cooking classes, food truck tastings, and celebrity chef appearances.

When: Usually in April.

Location: Scottsdale Civic Center Mall.

Cost: Tickets range from $50–$150 depending on event packages.

4. The Arizona Taco Festival (Scottsdale)

Description: If you're a taco lover, this festival is a must-attend. The Arizona Taco Festival celebrates the beloved taco with over 50 taco vendors offering their unique spins on this classic dish. From traditional to fusion tacos, you'll find a range of flavors to satisfy your cravings.

What to Expect: Taco competitions, taco-eating contests, live music, and a chance to sample a variety of tacos from around the world.

When: Typically held in October.

Location: Salt River Fields, Scottsdale.

Cost: $10–$25 per person; food available for purchase.

5. Chili Festival (Globe)

Description: The Chili Festival in Globe celebrates one of Arizona's most famous and spicy ingredients—chili. Whether you like it mild or fiery hot, this festival will delight chili lovers of all tastes. It features chili cook-offs, food booths, and even a chili-eating contest.

What to Expect: Chili cook-offs, local music, food vendors, and a family-friendly atmosphere.

When: Held every September.

Location: Downtown Globe.

Cost: Free entry; food and activities available for purchase.

Best Farmers' Markets in Arizona

Farmers' markets in Arizona offer an authentic taste of the state's agricultural richness, with opportunities to purchase fresh produce, homemade goods, and locally sourced products directly from farmers and artisans. Here are some of the best markets to visit:

1. The Downtown Phoenix Farmers Market (Phoenix)

Description: Open year-round, the Downtown Phoenix Farmers Market is one of the largest and most well-known markets in Arizona. With a strong emphasis on sustainability and local products, this market features fresh produce, locally made cheeses, baked goods, and artisanal products.

What to Expect: Organic produce, farm-fresh eggs, specialty foods, flowers, and local crafts.

When: Saturdays, 8:00 AM – 1:00 PM (Year-round).

Location: 721 N 1st Ave, Phoenix, AZ 85003.

Cost: Free entry; purchases vary in price.

2. Tempe Farmers Market & Artisan Market (Tempe)

Description: This market is known for its eclectic mix of fresh produce, handmade goods, and local artisan products. Visitors can also find a selection of food trucks offering delicious meals made from local ingredients.

What to Expect: Seasonal produce, locally made goods, hot food, baked goods, and live music.

When: Wednesdays and Saturdays, 8:00 AM – 1:00 PM.

Location: 805 S Farmer Ave, Tempe, AZ 85281.

Cost: Free entry; food and goods available for purchase.

3. Old Town Scottsdale Farmers Market (Scottsdale)

Description: This market offers a fantastic selection of fresh, locally grown produce, meats, and dairy products, as well as gourmet snacks and handcrafted goods. It's a great place to pick up ingredients for a meal or to enjoy a leisurely day of browsing.

What to Expect: Organic produce, grass-fed meats, farm-fresh eggs, and handmade products.

When: Saturdays, 8:00 AM – 1:00 PM (Year-round).

Location: 3806 N Brown Ave, Scottsdale, AZ 85251.

Cost: Free entry; food and goods available for purchase.

4. Flagstaff Community Market (Flagstaff)

Description: Open year-round, the Flagstaff Community Market is a favorite of locals and visitors alike. The market features an impressive array of local products, including meats, cheeses, and fresh produce, as well as handmade arts and crafts.

What to Expect: Local produce, meats, cheeses, baked goods, and homemade crafts.

When: Sundays, 8:00 AM – 1:00 PM (Year-round).

Location: 2401 N Fourth St, Flagstaff, AZ 86004.

Cost: Free entry; food and goods available for purchase.

5. Prescott Farmers Market (Prescott)

Description: Prescott's farmers market is a charming, community-focused market offering fresh and local produce, meats, and handmade products. It's a great place to stock up on local foods while supporting the regional economy.

What to Expect: Local produce, fresh flowers, meats, cheeses, and artisanal products.

When: Saturdays, 7:30 AM – 12:00 PM (May – November).

Location: 1001 Willow Creek Rd, Prescott, AZ 86301.

Cost: Free entry; food and goods available for purchase.

Enjoying the Flavors of Arizona

Food festivals and farmers' markets are a fantastic way to connect with Arizona's local communities, sample fresh and unique flavors, and learn about the state's agricultural traditions. Whether you're strolling through a bustling market in Phoenix or attending a lively food festival in Tucson, these experiences are sure to leave you with a deeper appreciation for Arizona's culinary culture.

Chapter 9: Travel Tips and Practical Information

9.1 Budgeting and Cost-Saving Tips

Traveling to Arizona can be an exciting adventure, but it's important to plan your budget wisely to make the most of your trip without overspending. Fortunately, Arizona offers a variety of affordable options for visitors to enjoy, from free outdoor activities to budget-friendly accommodations and dining options. Below are some helpful tips to help you save money while exploring the Grand Canyon State:

1. Travel During Off-Peak Seasons

One of the best ways to save money when visiting Arizona is by planning your trip during off-peak seasons. Arizona's peak travel months are typically in the spring (March to May) and fall (September to November), when the weather is mild, and outdoor activities are in full swing. However, these months also bring higher prices for hotels, attractions, and flights.

Best Off-Peak Seasons: Winter (December to February) and summer (June to August). While summer temperatures can soar in certain areas, there are plenty of indoor attractions and cooler spots like Flagstaff and the Grand Canyon to explore. Winter, on the other hand, can be great for lower hotel rates and fewer crowds at popular attractions.

2. Take Advantage of Free Attractions

Arizona is home to a wide range of natural beauty and cultural attractions that you can visit without spending a dime. Here are some budget-friendly ideas for exploring **Arizona's highlights:**

Hiking Trails: Arizona boasts some of the most stunning hiking trails in the country, many of which are free to access. Popular trails include those in Grand Canyon National Park, Sedona's Red Rocks, and Saguaro National Park.

State Parks: While entrance fees to state parks can vary, many parks offer low-cost entry, with beautiful vistas and unique geological features to enjoy. Slide Rock State Park and Red Rock State Park are two examples of affordable attractions.

Museums: While many museums charge admission, there are some in Arizona that offer free entry on certain days of the month. For instance, the Tucson Museum of Art and Arizona Capitol Museum offer free admission on specific days.

3. Save on Transportation

Transportation costs can add up quickly, but there are several ways to keep your travel expenses in check:

Public Transportation: Arizona's major cities, like Phoenix and Tucson, have affordable public transportation systems, including buses and light rail. Using public transport instead of renting a car can save you money, especially if you're only exploring the city.

Rent a Car Wisely: If you plan to rent a car, compare prices across multiple rental companies and book in advance to secure the best deal. Consider renting from a non-airport location, as airport rentals often have higher fees.

Carpool and Ride Shares: For those traveling within cities or smaller areas, using ride-share services like Uber or Lyft can be a more affordable option than renting a car or paying for parking.

4. Find Affordable Accommodations

Arizona offers a range of accommodations to fit different budgets. Whether you prefer camping under the stars or staying in a luxury resort, here are some tips to help you save on lodging:

Camping: Arizona is known for its vast natural spaces, and camping is an affordable way to experience the state's beauty. Many national forests, state parks, and campgrounds offer inexpensive camping sites. If you're visiting the Grand Canyon, there are several budget-friendly campsites within or near the park.

Hostels and Budget Hotels: If you're not into camping, Arizona has several affordable hostels and budget hotels, especially in cities like Phoenix, Tucson, and Flagstaff. Booking in advance or using booking websites to compare prices can help you find the best rates.

Vacation Rentals: Websites like Airbnb and Vrbo offer vacation rental options, which can often be more affordable than staying in hotels, especially for groups or families. Look for rentals in smaller towns or off-the-beaten-path areas for better prices.

5. Enjoy Affordable Dining

Arizona's food scene can be both delicious and affordable, especially if you know where to look. Here are some ways to save on food during your visit:

Eat Like a Local: Arizona has a thriving local food scene with many affordable, tasty options. Head to food trucks, local diners, and Mexican restaurants, where you can find generous portions at reasonable prices. Taco trucks and Mexican eateries are especially popular in Phoenix, Tucson, and Flagstaff.

Farmers' Markets: Shopping at Arizona's farmers' markets is a great way to get fresh, local produce at a fraction of the cost of grocery stores. You can often find inexpensive snacks, sandwiches, and pre-made meals at these markets, too.

Happy Hours: Many restaurants and bars in Arizona offer happy hour specials, which can be a great way to save on meals and drinks. You can often find discounted appetizers and drinks at popular spots in major cities.

6. Look for Deals and Discounts

Make sure to check for special deals and discounts before you travel to Arizona. Here are a few ways to find savings:

Arizona State Parks Pass: If you plan to visit multiple state parks, consider purchasing an annual pass. This pass gives you access to over 30 state parks and can save you money on entrance fees.

Discounted Attraction Tickets: Many popular attractions offer discounted tickets if purchased online in advance. Look for bundled ticket packages that combine multiple attractions at a reduced price.

Tourist Cards: Some cities, like Phoenix, offer tourist cards that provide discounts on popular attractions, dining, and tours.

7. Pack Smart and Avoid Extra Costs

Packing efficiently can help save you money on your trip. Here are a few packing tips to avoid unnecessary expenses:

Bring Reusable Water Bottles: Arizona's desert climate can get very hot, so it's essential to stay hydrated. Instead of buying bottled water, bring your own refillable water bottle to save money.

Pack for the Weather: Arizona's weather can vary widely depending on the region and the season. Packing the right clothes, including layers for cooler evenings and sunscreen for daytime, can prevent unnecessary purchases while you're traveling.

Avoid Excess Luggage Fees: If flying, pack light to avoid costly luggage fees. Many airlines charge for checked bags, so packing only carry-on luggage can help keep your costs down.

Conclusion

With careful planning, you can enjoy everything Arizona has to offer without breaking the bank. By taking advantage of free attractions, staying in affordable accommodations, saving on transportation, and seeking out discounts, you can make the most of your visit while keeping your expenses in check. Arizona is an amazing destination, and with a little budgeting, you can have an unforgettable experience without overspending.

9.2 Packing Advice for All Seasons

Packing for Arizona requires some thoughtful consideration, especially since the state offers a wide range of climates and activities depending on the season and location. Whether you're planning to explore the deserts, hike in the mountains, or experience the cities, here's how to pack efficiently for Arizona's ever-changing weather conditions:

1. Layer Your Clothing

Arizona's climate can be drastically different depending on where you are and the time of year. For example, while the deserts can be scorching hot during the day, the evenings can be chilly, especially in higher elevations. Therefore, layers are key to staying comfortable throughout the day:

Base Layer: Start with moisture-wicking clothing to keep sweat off your skin. This is especially important if you're planning outdoor activities like hiking.

Middle Layer: A lightweight fleece or jacket is great for cooler evenings, especially in mountainous areas like Sedona and Flagstaff.

Outer Layer: Depending on the season, a rain jacket or windbreaker will protect you from unexpected showers or windy conditions. A lightweight, breathable jacket is ideal during spring and fall.

2. Sun Protection

Arizona is known for its strong sunshine, and UV rays can be intense year-round, especially in the desert. Protecting your skin is crucial to avoid sunburns:

Sunscreen: Bring a high SPF sunscreen, and make sure to apply it every two hours, especially if you're spending time outdoors.

Hat: A wide-brimmed hat will protect your face and neck from the sun. Choose one with good ventilation to keep your head cool.

Sunglasses: Arizona's bright sun can cause eye strain, so pack UV-blocking sunglasses to protect your eyes while outdoors.

3. Footwear

Arizona's diverse landscapes call for different types of footwear. Here are some options based on what you'll be doing:

Hiking Shoes/Boots: If you plan to explore trails or visit national parks, be sure to pack durable hiking boots with ankle support. Arizona's terrain can be rocky and uneven, so it's important to have sturdy footwear for both comfort and safety.

Comfortable Walking Shoes: For sightseeing in the cities or relaxing in parks, a comfortable pair of sneakers or walking shoes is a must.

Sandals/Flip-Flops: During hot months, breathable sandals or flip-flops are ideal for lounging around or heading to the pool.

4. Seasonal Gear

Arizona has four distinct seasons, so your packing list should reflect the time of year you're visiting:

Spring: Light layers, sunscreen, and comfortable walking shoes will be sufficient. Arizona is known for its pleasant spring weather, perfect for hiking and sightseeing.

Summer: The summer months can be extremely hot, especially in desert regions like Phoenix and Scottsdale. Pack lightweight, breathable clothing, and bring extra water bottles, a hat, and sunglasses to keep cool.

Fall: This is one of the best times to visit, with crisp air and cooler evenings. Layers are key, and you can explore outdoor activities comfortably with light jackets and long-sleeved shirts.

Winter: If you're visiting higher elevations like Flagstaff or the Grand Canyon, be prepared for cold temperatures, especially at night. A heavier jacket, gloves, and a scarf may be necessary.

5. Essentials

Regardless of the season, be sure to pack these essential items for your **trip to Arizona:**

Water Bottle: Arizona's dry climate can cause dehydration quickly. Always carry a refillable water bottle to stay hydrated, especially when hiking or participating in outdoor activities.

Camera/Smartphone: With Arizona's stunning landscapes, you'll want to capture the beautiful scenery. A smartphone or a camera with a good zoom lens is perfect for snapping pictures of the deserts, canyons, and red rocks.

First-Aid Kit: Having a small first-aid kit with bandages, antiseptic wipes, and pain relievers can be a lifesaver, especially if you're hiking or exploring remote areas.

Chargers and Power Bank: Always keep your phone charged for navigation, photography, and emergency situations. A portable power bank can be very helpful on long excursions.

6. Packing Light

While Arizona offers many opportunities for adventure, it's best to pack as light as possible, especially if you plan to be active. Keep your luggage manageable to ensure a stress-free trip, and avoid packing unnecessary items. A good rule of thumb is to bring only what you need and be prepared to do laundry if you're staying for a longer period.

9.3 Staying Safe Outdoors and in Town

Whether you're exploring the stunning landscapes of Arizona's deserts and mountains or immersing yourself in the vibrant cities, staying safe should always be a top priority. Arizona's diverse terrain and climate mean that different areas require different precautions. Here are some key safety tips for both outdoor adventures and urban exploration:

1. Outdoor Safety

Arizona's outdoor spaces are breathtaking, but they can also pose risks, especially during extreme weather conditions. Here's how to stay safe when enjoying the great outdoors:

Stay Hydrated: The desert heat, especially in summer, can be intense. Always carry plenty of water with you, particularly when hiking or exploring remote areas. Dehydration is a serious risk in Arizona, and water should always be your top priority.

Know the Terrain: Before heading out, familiarize yourself with the area. Arizona's wilderness areas, including national parks and remote trails, can be challenging, so it's important to understand the terrain, difficulty levels, and landmarks. Use maps, GPS apps, and check trail conditions ahead of time.

Check the Weather: Arizona's weather can be unpredictable, especially during summer monsoon season (July to September), which brings sudden thunderstorms and flash flooding. Always check the forecast and be prepared to change your plans if the weather turns bad.

Avoid Sunburn: The Arizona sun is intense, and you can burn quickly. Apply sunscreen liberally, wear protective clothing, and avoid direct exposure to the sun between noon and 3 p.m. when UV rays are strongest.

Be Mindful of Wildlife: Arizona is home to a variety of wildlife, including snakes, scorpions, and mountain lions. While these creatures are generally not aggressive, it's important to stay alert. Keep a safe distance from any wild animals and avoid disturbing them. Wear protective shoes and be cautious when hiking in rocky areas.

Know Emergency Numbers: Familiarize yourself with emergency numbers for the area, especially if you're venturing into remote or less populated regions. In Arizona, dial 911 for emergencies.

2. Urban Safety

Arizona's cities, such as Phoenix and Tucson, offer exciting urban experiences, but it's still important to be cautious, especially in busy areas. Here are some tips for staying safe in the city:

Watch Your Belongings: As with any major city, it's important to be mindful of your personal items. Avoid leaving valuables unattended, especially in public spaces. Use a money belt or secure pouch for things like credit cards, passports, and cash.

Stay in Well-Lit Areas: When walking around in the evening, choose well-lit areas and stay on main streets. Avoid walking alone late at night in unfamiliar or poorly lit neighborhoods.

Use Public Transportation Safely: Arizona's cities have public transit systems, but always stay aware of your surroundings. If you're using a rideshare service, check that the car's details match the information provided in the app, and confirm the driver's identity before getting in.

Follow Local Guidelines: In larger cities, it's important to stay informed about local laws and guidelines, especially regarding parking, alcohol consumption, and outdoor activities. Respecting these rules will ensure that your experience is safe and enjoyable.

Know the Local Emergency Services: In addition to 911, it's useful to have the contact information for local police, medical services, and fire departments if you're traveling in urban areas. Many hotels provide this information at the front desk.

By following these safety tips, you can enjoy your time in Arizona with peace of mind, whether you're in the wild or exploring the vibrant cities. Stay prepared, stay aware, and always put safety first.

9.4 Road Safety and Wilderness Etiquette

Arizona's wide-open roads and vast wilderness areas offer incredible opportunities for exploration. However, it's important to follow road safety rules and wilderness etiquette to ensure that your adventures are both safe and respectful of the environment and other travelers. Here are some key tips to keep in mind while on the road and in nature:

1. Road Safety

Arizona is known for its long highways, scenic byways, and rural roads, making it a great place for road trips. However, some areas may have challenging driving conditions. Follow these tips to stay safe on the **road:**

Watch for Wildlife: Arizona is home to a variety of wildlife, including deer, javelinas, and even mountain lions. Be especially cautious when driving at dawn or dusk, when animals are most active. Slow down and use your headlights if you're driving in rural or forested areas.

Drive for the Conditions: Arizona's weather can change quickly, especially in mountainous areas. Heavy rains during the monsoon season (typically from July to September) can lead to slick roads and flash floods. Always reduce speed during bad weather and avoid driving through flooded areas. If snow is forecasted in the higher elevations, be prepared for slippery conditions and carry tire chains if necessary.

Stay on the Roads: Arizona has vast desert landscapes, and it may be tempting to take your vehicle off-road. However, driving off designated paths can damage fragile ecosystems and is illegal in many areas. Always stick to marked roads and trails to protect the environment.

Follow Speed Limits: Speed limits can vary widely in Arizona, so always check posted signs, especially in rural areas. Some highways may have long stretches without intersections or traffic, but it's still important to obey speed limits for your safety and the safety of others.

Fuel Up: Arizona has large expanses of wilderness, especially in the northern and southern parts of the state. Gas stations can be few and far between in these areas. Be sure to fill up your tank whenever you have the chance, and keep an eye on your fuel gauge, particularly if you're heading into remote areas.

Keep Emergency Supplies: Always have a roadside emergency kit with items like water, a first-aid kit, flashlight, extra clothing, and non-perishable snacks. If you break down or get stuck in a remote area, this kit can be a lifesaver.

2. Wilderness Etiquette

When exploring Arizona's stunning national parks, deserts, forests, and wilderness areas, it's essential to respect the environment, wildlife, and fellow visitors. Follow these wilderness etiquette guidelines to ensure a positive experience for everyone:

Leave No Trace: Arizona's natural landscapes are a treasure, and it's important to minimize your impact. Always follow Leave No Trace principles by packing out all trash, staying on designated trails, and leaving nature undisturbed. Avoid picking plants or disturbing wildlife.

Respect Wildlife: While it's tempting to approach wildlife for a closer look or a photo, remember that animals can be dangerous if provoked. Always maintain a safe distance from wildlife, and never feed them. Feeding wildlife can alter their natural behaviors and create dangerous situations.

Be Quiet in Nature: Arizona's wilderness areas provide solitude and peace for visitors. Keep noise to a minimum, especially when camping or hiking. Loud music or shouting can disturb both wildlife and other visitors, detracting from the experience for everyone.

Follow Trail Rules: When hiking, biking, or walking in nature, follow trail rules and regulations. Stick to marked paths to avoid damaging fragile ecosystems, and yield the trail to others when necessary, especially on narrow paths.

Respect Campground Rules: If you're camping, adhere to the rules of the campsite. Respect quiet hours, keep campfires within designated fire rings, and never leave fires unattended. Always extinguish fires completely before leaving.

9.5 Language Tips and Local Customs

Although Arizona is an English-speaking state, there are a few unique language tips and local customs that can help you connect with residents and enhance your travel experience. Knowing these small details can make your visit to Arizona more enjoyable and respectful of the local culture.

1. Language and Communication

English is Predominant: English is the primary language spoken in Arizona, so communication won't be a problem for most visitors. However, you may hear some

Spanish spoken in areas with a large Hispanic population, especially in southern Arizona and near the Mexican border.

Spanish Phrases: Knowing a few basic Spanish phrases can be helpful, especially in Tucson, Yuma, and other border cities. Here are some **simple phrases to learn:**

"Hola" – Hello

"Gracias" – Thank you

"¿Dónde está...?" – Where is...?

"Por favor" – Please

"Adiós" – Goodbye

"¿Cuánto cuesta?" – How much does it cost?

Local Dialects and Terms: In addition to Spanish, Arizona's local dialect may include some colloquial expressions and terms related to the culture. For example, "Y'all" (a Southern expression meaning "you all") is often heard in Arizona, especially in rural areas.

2. Local Customs and Etiquette

Understanding local customs will help you blend in and make your trip more enjoyable. Here are a few tips about Arizona's culture and etiquette:

Hospitality: Arizona residents are known for their warm hospitality. It's common to greet people with a friendly "hello" or "howdy," especially in smaller towns or rural areas. Don't be surprised if locals engage in small talk, even with strangers.

Punctuality: In larger cities like Phoenix and Tucson, punctuality is important for business meetings and appointments. However, in smaller, rural towns, the pace of life is more relaxed, and people may not be as strict about timeliness.

Respect for Native American Culture: Arizona is home to many Native American tribes, and it's essential to show respect for their culture and history. Be mindful of sacred sites and always ask for permission before taking photographs in Native American communities. If you visit tribal lands, follow any specific rules set by the tribe.

Tipping: Tipping is customary in Arizona and follows the same guidelines as in most of the United States:

Restaurants: 15-20% of the total bill is typical.

Hotel Staff: Tip bellhops $1-2 per bag, and leave $2-5 per night for housekeeping.

Taxis/Rideshare: A 10-15% tip is customary for taxi drivers or rideshare drivers.

Respect for Nature: Arizona residents deeply appreciate the state's natural beauty, and it's important to show respect for the land by following Leave No Trace principles. Whether you're hiking, camping, or exploring national parks, always treat nature with care.

By understanding and embracing these language tips and local customs, you'll have a more immersive and respectful experience while traveling in Arizona. Whether you're enjoying a lively city or the quiet desert, showing kindness and consideration will make your trip more rewarding.

.

Chapter 10: FAQs and Additional Resources

10.1 Frequently Asked Questions for Visitors

Planning a trip to Arizona can bring up a lot of questions. Whether you're visiting for the first time or returning for another adventure, we've compiled a list of frequently asked questions to help you plan your visit. These FAQs cover everything from weather and transportation to accommodations and safety tips.

1. What is the best time of year to visit Arizona?
The best time to visit Arizona depends on what you want to do.
Spring (March to May) is ideal for outdoor activities like hiking and sightseeing, as temperatures are warm but not too hot.
Fall (September to November) is another great time to visit because the weather is pleasant, especially for exploring Arizona's desert landscapes.
Summer (June to August) can be very hot, especially in the southern parts of the state, but it's a good time to visit higher-altitude locations like Flagstaff or the Grand Canyon.
Winter (December to February) is perfect if you're looking for cooler weather and want to experience skiing or snowboarding in places like Flagstaff or the White Mountains.

2. How hot does it get in Arizona during the summer?
Arizona is known for its hot summers, especially in the southern and central parts of the state. In places like Phoenix and Tucson, temperatures can easily exceed 100°F (38°C) in June, July, and August. However, northern Arizona, including places like Sedona and the Grand Canyon, tends to be much cooler, with daytime temperatures in the 70s and 80s°F (21-27°C). It's essential to stay hydrated and avoid outdoor activities during the hottest parts of the day.

3. Are there any dangerous animals in Arizona?
Yes, Arizona is home to a few animals that can be dangerous if encountered. These include:
Rattlesnakes: Found in many parts of Arizona, especially during the warmer months. Always stay on marked trails and watch where you step.

Scorpions: Common in desert areas. Be cautious when camping or staying in rural areas.

Mountain Lions: Though sightings are rare, they live in Arizona's mountains and forests. If you encounter one, make yourself appear larger and slowly back away.

Despite these risks, most wildlife in Arizona is not a threat if you follow safety guidelines and remain aware of your surroundings.

4. How can I avoid the heat when visiting Arizona?

To stay cool and avoid the heat in Arizona:

Drink plenty of water: Stay hydrated throughout the day.

Wear sunscreen: Apply sunscreen with a high SPF, and wear protective clothing like hats and sunglasses.

Take breaks indoors: Visit museums, galleries, or shopping malls during the hottest parts of the day (usually 10 AM to 4 PM).

Go for early or late hikes: If you're hiking or exploring outdoors, do so early in the morning or later in the evening when temperatures are cooler.

Visit higher-altitude areas: Northern Arizona and places like Flagstaff and the Grand Canyon have cooler temperatures, even in the summer.

5. What are the top attractions in Arizona?

Some of Arizona's top attractions include:

Grand Canyon National Park: One of the most famous natural wonders in the world.

Sedona: Known for its stunning red rock formations and outdoor activities.

Monument Valley: Iconic desert landscapes and Native American culture.

Saguaro National Park: Home to the unique saguaro cactus and beautiful desert views.

Phoenix and Tucson: Bustling cities with museums, shopping, and nearby natural beauty.

6. Can I visit the Grand Canyon year-round?

Yes, the Grand Canyon is open year-round, but the experience can vary depending on the season. In winter, the South Rim can experience snow, offering a quieter, more peaceful experience with fewer crowds. Summer is the peak tourist season, so expect larger crowds and warmer temperatures. The North Rim is closed in winter, typically from mid-October to mid-May, due to snow and weather conditions.

7. What should I pack for a trip to Arizona?

What you pack for Arizona depends on when and where you're visiting. Here's a general packing guide:

For summer: Lightweight clothing, sunscreen, sunglasses, a hat, comfortable shoes, and plenty of water.

For winter: A jacket (it can get chilly, especially in northern Arizona), layers, and comfortable shoes for walking.

For hiking: Sturdy hiking boots, a backpack, a first-aid kit, water, and a hat for sun protection.

For the desert: Bring a bandana or scarf to protect your face from dust and sand, and a camera to capture the scenic beauty.

8. Are there public transportation options in Arizona?

Public transportation options in Arizona are available but limited, especially outside major cities.

Phoenix and Tucson have bus systems and light rail that can help you get around the city.

Sedona and smaller towns may require you to rent a car or rely on local shuttle services.

For long-distance travel, you can take Greyhound buses or Amtrak trains to reach different parts of the state.

In remote areas, renting a car is typically the best option for getting around.

9. Can I visit Arizona's national parks during the holidays?

Yes, Arizona's national parks are open during the holidays, though some services may be limited, especially on major holidays like Christmas and New Year's. It's always a good idea to check the specific park's website or call ahead to confirm operating hours, visitor center availability, and any special events happening during the holidays.

10. Is Arizona a family-friendly destination?

Yes, Arizona is a fantastic destination for families. From the Grand Canyon to the Desert Museum in Tucson, and fun activities like horseback riding, jeep tours, and visits to Native American cultural sites, Arizona offers plenty of family-friendly experiences. Many hotels, resorts, and parks offer family-friendly amenities, and there are numerous activities to keep kids entertained while also engaging in educational experiences.

By answering these common questions, we hope to help make your trip to Arizona easier and more enjoyable. Whether you're hiking in the desert, exploring the vibrant culture, or relaxing by the pool, Arizona has something to offer every traveler.

10.2 Maps, Apps, and Travel Tools

Having the right tools and resources can make navigating Arizona much easier, especially when you're exploring the state's vast and varied landscapes. Whether you're heading into the desert, hiking a mountain, or exploring city streets, these maps, apps, and tools can help you get around, stay on track, and make the most of your visit.

Maps

Arizona State Map: A physical or downloadable map of Arizona is a great resource for general navigation. You can pick up a free state map at most visitor centers or online at the Arizona Office of Tourism website.

National Park Maps: Most national parks, including the Grand Canyon and Saguaro National Park, offer detailed maps that you can download or pick up at entrance stations. These maps are crucial for hiking trails, scenic viewpoints, and emergency exits.

Topographic Maps: If you're planning to hike in Arizona's mountains or deserts, a detailed topographic map can be invaluable. These maps show the elevation, terrain, and route options for hiking and camping. Look for topographic maps on websites like AllTrails or through GPS mapping apps.

Apps

Google Maps: A must-have for general navigation. It works well in both urban areas like Phoenix and Tucson, as well as more remote parts of the state. Be sure to download offline maps of areas with limited signal.

AllTrails: If you're into hiking or nature walks, AllTrails is an excellent app to discover trail information, reviews, and maps for hundreds of Arizona trails, including the Grand Canyon and Sedona's red rocks.

Roadtrippers: This app helps you plan road trips and discover interesting stops along the way, including scenic routes, quirky roadside attractions, and natural wonders across Arizona.

Arizona State Parks App: This app provides information on state parks across Arizona, including entry fees, park maps, and seasonal alerts.

Avenza Maps: Great for offline mapping, Avenza lets you download high-quality topographic maps and other outdoor-specific maps that you can use without cell service.

Other Travel Tools

ParkPasses and Tickets: Many of Arizona's most popular national parks, like the Grand Canyon and Saguaro, require entry passes. You can buy these online at the official park websites or use the America the Beautiful National Parks Pass for access to over 2,000 federal recreation sites.

Weather Apps: Arizona's weather can vary drastically, especially when traveling between elevations. Apps like The Weather Channel or AccuWeather are good for real-time updates, including temperature, rainfall, and alerts for extreme weather conditions.

Road Conditions: If you're driving through Arizona's more remote areas, it's important to know road conditions before you go. The Arizona Department of Transportation (ADOT) website offers real-time updates on road closures, construction zones, and other road hazards.

10.3 Key Emergency Contacts and Numbers

It's essential to be prepared in case of an emergency while traveling. Arizona's diverse landscapes present unique situations, so having the right contacts on hand can be life-saving in case of an accident, medical issue, or any unexpected event.

General Emergency Numbers

Emergency (Police, Fire, Ambulance): 911

This is the universal emergency number in Arizona for all types of emergencies, including medical, fire, and police. Make sure your phone is charged and accessible when exploring remote areas.

Arizona Poison and Drug Information

Center: 1-800-222-1222

If you are in need of medical help due to poisoning or drug-related issues, this is the number to call for assistance from trained specialists.

Local Police and Sheriffs

Phoenix Police Department: 602-262-6151

Tucson Police Department: 520-791-4444

Flagstaff Police Department: 928-774-1414

Sedona Police Department: 928-282-3100

Grand Canyon National Park Rangers (Emergency): 928-638-7805

Medical Services

Grand Canyon Emergency Services: 928-638-2477

For immediate help inside the Grand Canyon, this is the emergency medical number for the park's South Rim area.

Banner Health (Phoenix Area): 602-839-6000

Banner Health has multiple locations across the state, including emergency rooms, urgent care centers, and specialty services.

Tucson Medical Center: 520-694-0111

This hospital is the largest in southern Arizona, with emergency services available 24/7.

Sedona Medical Center: 928-282-4323

For medical emergencies or health concerns while visiting Sedona, this is the closest hospital to the town.

Medical Transportation (Air Ambulance):

If you're visiting remote areas or engaging in outdoor activities, it's helpful to know that services like Air Evac Lifeteam (800-793-0010) provide air ambulance transportation in case of emergency.

Visitor Services and Helplines

Arizona Tourism Hotline: 1-877-698-9494

This number provides information on events, attractions, accommodations, and travel tips across the state. The Arizona Office of Tourism also offers resources for navigating public lands and accessing visitor centers.

National Park Service (Grand Canyon & Other Parks): 928-638-7888

For park-specific inquiries, including trails, closures, and general visitor information at the Grand Canyon, this number can connect you to the park service.

Arizona Department of Transportation (Road Conditions): 511

Dial 511 for updates on road conditions, traffic alerts, accidents, and closures in Arizona. You can also visit the ADOT website for detailed information.

U.S. Forest Service (Camping and Hiking): 1-877-444-6777

If you need information about national forests, campgrounds, or hiking conditions across Arizona, this is the helpline to call.

Medical Insurance and Travel Assistance

Travel Insurance Companies: Make sure you have travel insurance to cover emergencies like medical issues, trip cancellations, or lost luggage. Some well-known companies that cover Arizona travel are:

World Nomads: 1-800-219-9336

Travel Guard: 1-800-826-1300

Local Hospitals and Urgent Care

Urgent Care Locations: Many cities, including Phoenix and Tucson, have urgent care centers available for non-emergency medical needs. A simple search on Google Maps or Yelp will help you find the nearest urgent care facility in the area you're visiting.

By keeping these emergency contacts and tools handy, you can ensure that you're prepared for any situation while visiting Arizona. It's always a good idea to have important numbers saved on your phone and carry a physical copy of essential contact information, just in case you lose signal or your phone battery dies. Stay safe, and enjoy everything Arizona has to offer!

10.4 Sustainable and Eco-Friendly Travel Tips

Traveling in an eco-conscious way is increasingly important as more people explore Arizona's beautiful landscapes. From the desert to the mountains, Arizona's natural wonders rely on protection and care, and as visitors, we can do our part to minimize our environmental impact. Here are some sustainable and eco-friendly travel tips for your Arizona trip:

1. Stick to Designated Trails and Roads

When hiking or exploring Arizona's outdoor spaces, always stay on marked trails and roads to avoid disturbing delicate ecosystems. Off-roading and wandering off designated paths can damage the desert soil and disturb local wildlife habitats. Most national parks and state parks have well-maintained trails, so make sure you follow them to preserve Arizona's pristine nature.

2. Reduce Water Usage

Arizona is a desert state, so water is a valuable resource. Be mindful of your water usage, especially in rural areas. Try to minimize shower time, avoid leaving the tap running, and consider using reusable water bottles. Some locations may have water refill stations, so bring your own bottle to reduce plastic waste.

3. Choose Eco-Friendly Accommodations

Many hotels, lodges, and resorts in Arizona are adopting sustainable practices, such as using renewable energy sources, recycling programs, and water conservation efforts. Look for eco-friendly accommodations, such as LEED-certified hotels or those with a clear sustainability policy. These places often use energy-efficient lighting, eco-friendly cleaning products, and participate in water and waste reduction initiatives.

4. Support Local and Sustainable Businesses

Shopping and dining locally help minimize your carbon footprint by reducing the environmental impact of shipping goods over long distances. Look for restaurants and markets that prioritize locally sourced ingredients and sustainable farming practices. Similarly, when purchasing souvenirs, choose locally made products instead of mass-produced goods that may harm the environment.

5. Bring Reusable Items

Bring your own reusable bags, containers, and utensils to minimize single-use plastic waste. Arizona's outdoor areas are often impacted by litter, so carrying your own reusable items, such as a coffee cup or shopping bag, can make a difference. If you do use disposable items, make sure to dispose of them properly or recycle them if possible.

6. Respect Wildlife

Arizona is home to a variety of wildlife, including bighorn sheep, mountain lions, and desert tortoises. When encountering animals, maintain a safe distance and never feed them. Feeding wildlife disrupts their natural behaviors and can be harmful to both the animals and humans. Respect local wildlife by not disturbing their habitats.

7. Participate in Environmental Programs

Many Arizona parks and organizations offer opportunities for visitors to help with conservation efforts. Look out for volunteering programs, like trash clean-ups or tree-planting events, during your visit. Participating in such activities not only helps preserve Arizona's natural beauty but also makes you feel more connected to the environment.

8. Use Public Transport or Carpool

To reduce your carbon footprint, use public transportation or carpool when possible. Arizona's urban areas like Phoenix and Tucson have bus systems that are affordable and environmentally friendly. Additionally, if you're visiting popular tourist sites, consider sharing rides with other travelers to cut down on the number of vehicles on the road.

By following these simple tips, you'll help protect Arizona's stunning landscapes and preserve them for future generations. Sustainable travel isn't just a trend—it's a responsibility we all share.

10.5 Arizona Itineraries for 3, 5, and 7-Day Trips

Whether you have three days or a full week, Arizona offers something for everyone, from breathtaking national parks to vibrant cities and charming small towns. Here are suggested itineraries to help you make the most of your time in Arizona:

3-Day Arizona Itinerary: Best of the Desert and Mountains

Day 1: Grand Canyon National Park

Start your journey with the iconic Grand Canyon. Spend your day exploring the South Rim, taking in panoramic views, and walking along the rim trails. Don't miss the sunset, which offers a stunning view of the canyon's vibrant colors.

Optional: Take a scenic helicopter ride over the canyon for a unique perspective.

Day 2: Sedona and Red Rock Country

After the Grand Canyon, head south to Sedona (2.5-hour drive). Explore the famous red rock formations and take a hike to Cathedral Rock or Devil's Bridge. If you're up for it, take a Jeep tour for an off-road adventure.

In the evening, relax at one of Sedona's excellent restaurants or enjoy stargazing in this dark-sky community.

Day 3: Phoenix and the Valley of the Sun

Spend your last day in Arizona exploring Phoenix, the state's largest city. Visit the Heard Museum to learn about Native American art and culture. Take a hike up Camelback Mountain for sweeping views of the city, or visit Desert Botanical Garden to see unique desert plant life.

5-Day Arizona Itinerary: Exploring Nature and Culture

Day 1: Grand Canyon National Park

Begin with a full day at the Grand Canyon, with a hike into the canyon or a visit to the museum. You can also take a scenic drive along the Desert View Drive.

Day 2: Monument Valley and Navajo Nation

Drive to Monument Valley (3.5-hour drive from the Grand Canyon), a stunning landscape featured in countless Western films. Take a guided tour with a Navajo guide to learn about the area's history and culture.

Day 3: Sedona and Oak Creek Canyon

Head to Sedona (2.5-hour drive) to explore the red rocks, take a jeep tour, and visit the Chapel of the Holy Cross, an architectural wonder set into the rocks. In the afternoon, drive through the picturesque Oak Creek Canyon for more natural beauty.

Day 4: Tucson and Southern Arizona

Spend the day in Tucson (2.5-hour drive), exploring Saguaro National Park, where you can hike among the giant saguaro cacti. Visit the Arizona-Sonora Desert Museum to learn about desert wildlife and enjoy a sunset at Gates Pass.

Day 5: Phoenix and Departure

On your final day, stop in Phoenix to visit the Desert Botanical Garden or take a walk through the Desert Ridge Marketplace before catching your flight home.

7-Day Arizona Itinerary: The Ultimate Grand Adventure

Day 1: Grand Canyon National Park

Begin with a full day at the Grand Canyon. Hike the South Kaibab Trail or take the shuttle to the North Rim for a different perspective.

Day 2: Sedona and Red Rock Country

Drive to Sedona (2.5-hour drive) and spend your day hiking, shopping, and visiting the Sedona Arts Center. In the evening, enjoy a relaxing dinner with a view of the red rocks.

Day 3: Monument Valley and Navajo Nation

Spend the day at Monument Valley, taking a guided tour through the stunning desert landscape and learning about Navajo traditions.

Day 4: Tucson and Southern Arizona

Head to Tucson (3-hour drive) to explore the desert and visit the University of Arizona's Mineral Museum. Stop by the Pima Air & Space Museum or spend some time at the historic downtown.

Day 5: Phoenix and the Valley of the Sun

In Phoenix, visit the Heard Museum or take a hike up Camelback Mountain. Explore the local shops and dine at one of the city's farm-to-table restaurants.

Day 6: Lake Mead and Hoover Dam

Take a day trip to Lake Mead (4-hour drive) and the Hoover Dam (1 hour from

Phoenix), where you can take a boat tour on the lake or walk across the dam and learn about its history.

Day 7: Departure

Spend your final day shopping for souvenirs or relaxing at a spa in Scottsdale before heading home.

These itineraries offer a mix of Arizona's best attractions, from the iconic Grand Canyon to cultural hotspots like Sedona and Tucson. Whether you have a short stay or an extended vacation, Arizona has something for every type of traveler.

Acknowledgments and Feedback
Acknowledgments:

We would like to extend our heartfelt gratitude to all those who made this Arizona Travel Guide possible. A special thanks to the many locals, tour guides, park rangers, and hospitality professionals across the state, who shared their expertise and helped us craft this guide with accuracy and enthusiasm. Without their insights, this book would not have been as thorough or enjoyable to read.

We also wish to acknowledge the numerous photographers whose captivating images of Arizona's landscapes, wildlife, and cultural heritage enriched this book. Their work brought the beauty of Arizona to life in a way that words alone cannot.

Lastly, a big thank you to our dedicated team of writers, editors, and designers who worked tirelessly to ensure that this guide provides an informative and inspiring resource for travelers.

Providing Feedback:

We truly value the feedback of our readers, as it helps us improve and refine future editions. If you have visited Arizona and used this guide, we'd love to hear about your experiences and any suggestions you may have. Whether you have recommendations on hidden gems, additional travel tips, or comments on the guide itself, your input will help make this resource even better for future travelers.

To provide feedback or share your thoughts:

Email Us: You can reach us at email@example.com.

Visit Our Website: For the latest updates and to share your feedback, visit our website at www.aztravelguide.com.

Follow Us on Social Media: Join our community and share your adventures in Arizona using the hashtag #AZTravelGuide on platforms like Instagram, Facebook, and Twitter.

Your feedback ensures that we continue to offer the most current, accurate, and useful information for travelers eager to explore the Grand Canyon State.

Thank you for your support, and we wish you an unforgettable journey through Arizona!

Made in United States
Troutdale, OR
03/07/2025

29551241R00080